D1276355

Excesses: Eros and Culture

excesses

eros and culture

alphonso lingis

State University of New York Press
Albany

A part of "Savages" appeared in *Semiotexte,* Vol. III, No. 2, 1978.

An early version of "The Rangda" appeared in *Philosophy and Literature,* Vol. IV, No. 1, Spring 1980.

An early version of "Khajuraho" appeared in *Soundings:* An Interdisciplinary Journal, Vol. LXII, No. 1, Spring 1979.

The photograph facing Chapter 2 is courtesy of Leni Riefenstahl. First published in Leni Riefenstahl, *The Last of the Nuba* (New York: Harper & Row), 1973.

Published by
State University of New York Press, Albany

© 1983 State University of New York

All rights reserved

Printed in the United States of America

No part of this book may be used or reproduced in any manner whatsoever without written permission except in the case of brief quotations embodied in critical articles and reviews.

For information, address State University of New York Press, State University Plaza, Albany, N.Y., 12246

Library of Congress Cataloging in Publication Data

Lingis, Alphonso, 1933–
   Excesses: eros and culture

   1. Sex (Psychology)—Social aspects. 2. Sex
customs. I. Title.
BF692.L54 1984   306.7   83-9122
ISBN 0-87395-797-0
ISBN 0-87395-796-2 (pbk.)

10 9 8 7 6 5 4 3 2 1

On the other hand, we hold that Sade's bedroom is the equal of those places from which the schools of ancient philosophy took their names —Academy, Lyceum, Stoa. Here, as there, science was being prepared through a rectification of the position of ethics.

Jacques Lacan, *"Kant avec Sade"*

Contents

Illustrations

Preface

FREUD LIBERATED SEXUALITY FROM THE BIOLOGICAL FINALITY IN which it is normally envisaged—without directing all the nonreproductive energies of eroticism into the production of pleasure for the individual. For psychoanalysis has but a weak concept of the individual.

There are excesses in sexuality; indeed the libido is the name Freud, Nietzsche, and Bataille have taught us to use to cover the excess in the artifices of life.

In this book I set out to explore the impulses—the excessive impulses—of our eroticism in new ways, in remote places.

I first show how I came to think that the craving and longing in eros are not really cravings of the I, longings for the I. The dismembered and voluptuous eye seeks, in the deep, for the look of the other.

In East Africa I saw the primary process libido inscribed on the surfaces, producing surface and ephemeral egos.

In Khajuraho, in medieval India, I came to distinguish three kinds of sublimation.

In Bali I found a solar version of the death drive.

In the New Guinea highlands, I found a cannibalism that was not the inauguration of civilization, that is, in Freud's terms, of castration.

In a Tantric ritual witnessed in Sri Lanka, I saw a face of sovereignty. Not the sovereignty of the person, but of the compassionate no-self, eyes open upon the universal impermanence.

What then would be the association of men who are not civilized, that is, not determined by instinctual renunciation, not castrated, not tooled for one another, not agents of an exchange economy? At the end of the book I thought about that, thought about six encounters in the East where contact was made across the most remote social distances.

The Rapture of the Deep

Full fathom five thy father lies;
Of his bones are coral made;
Those are pearls that were his eyes:
Nothing of him that doth fade,
But doth suffer a sea-change
Into something rich and strange.
Shakespeare, *The Tempest*

CAN WE, SPACEMEN, STILL BE SAID TO LIVE IN A WORLD? A world is not simply the sum total of all the things, implements, pathways, impedimenta there are. A world, a cosmos, is the order, the ordinance, extending according to axes of close and far, intimate and alien, upwards and downwards, lofty and base, right and left, auspicious and inauspicious, within which things can have their places, show their aspects and stake out paths. A world can not be perceived or manipulated as the things can. For generations of men before us, the coordinates of a world were marked in temples. Temples fix the directions to immanence and to the beyond, to the sublime and to the ignoble, to grandeur and to malediction. With the ruin of temples, the worlds they opened turns into homogeneous space, where up and down, far and close, left and right are interchangeable, axes of the et cetera ad infinitum. Why now go down the gorges of the Rift Valley where *homo habilis* first arose four million years ago, why climb again the Himalayas, why go oneself to the Stone Age highlands of New Guinea? One does go still, to be sure, to the far end of the planet in a few hours by jet airplane, to dine at an Intercontinental Hotel in Kathmandu or on the beaches of Bali, or one goes nowhere and sees the same, indeed better, guided by experts, the sanctuaries of the forbidden city and the incantations of aborigines in one's own living room, close as the television screen.

3

What more did he learn, the one who unreasonably spent the weeks to cross Afghanistan to go himself look at some dust-covered ruins, to listen to the unintelligible jabbering of doubtful information by a cloying local guide whose cupidity attaching him to the foreigner was the sole instinct left on the debris of what had been wrought by sublime compulsions and visionary will? What does one have to tell, but of the dust-choked lungs, the amoebic dysenteries, the unsleeping nights on vermin-ridden cots, the incomprehension, encounters with the hopeless horrors of hunger-dulled eyes and leprous hands? What has one to tell, but the pain?

What will one have to tell, having gone down oneself, strapped with iron weights and the steel gills of an aqualung and gauges to warn of the forbidden depths and pressures, of nitrogen narcosis, pneumothorax, air embolisms, to go paddle for an hour among the coral fish? When one comes back one will learn their names and their ways from books and sit with the others to watch Cousteau films on television.

Why did one also crave to embrace and couple with strangers? What else did one get in orgasms, which one did not get through commerce with the other in the exchange systems of economy, marriage, language?

Still there is the compulsion to travel the Ganges, to return to the oceans, some kind of resentment against the Intercontinental Hotels and instant Asia, and even against the long fathomless sagacity of life that contrived the organism to walk upright on land. Reversing ontogenesis to reverse phylogenesis. That thalassa complex, which, according to Ferenczi, is the libido itself. "The purpose of the sex act can be none other than an attempt on the part of the ego—an attempt at the beginning clumsy and fumbling, then more consciously purposive, and finally in part successful—to return to the mother's womb... The sex act achieves this transitory regression in a threefold manner: the whole organism attains this goal by purely hallucinatory means, somewhat as in sleep; the penis with which the organism as a whole has identified itself attains it partially or symbolically; while only the sexual secretion possesses the prerogative, as representative of the ego and its narcissistic double, the genitalia, of attaining in reality to the womb of the mother." What reaches the briney womb is this plankton in which one voluptuously compresses everything of oneself. The compulsion to copulate— parental compulsion, that takes responsibility for the future of the species on the earth—is also what is most infantile, compulsion to regress to the infancy of all life, compulsion to return from the fixed paths of every world to the oceanic womb—to find oneself where? In the cosmic axes? In depth itself? "Since the individual identifies himself with the phallus inserted in the vagina and with the spermatozoa swarming into the body of the female, he also repeats symbolically the danger of death which his animal ancestors victor- iously overcame in the geological cataclysms of the drying up of the sea."[1]

Laden with air tank, regulator, gauges, I went into the sea. The belt of iron weights dropped me through the strong current of the surface. Below there was no current, but there was surge, water compressed to three atmospheres throwing me back and forth thirty feet, so that I fought it violently to stabilize myself, afraid of being dashed against the coral cliffs. Something then told me to put off struggling, to free my body from human posture and swim strokes, to use my limbs only like some thalidomide freak able to make but the slight movements necessary to avoid the prongs of elkhorn coral and steer into canyons. The fish accompanied me then, stable in the surge, part of the surge. I drowned the will to move myself, consigned myself to the movement of—what? Equatorial storms that had not been visible on the surface, that were raging or had raged perhaps hundreds of miles away? Earthquakes or volcanic cataclysms breaking the floors of the abyss? The movement of the moon swinging in its orbit two hundred and forty thousand miles away? And then the bliss came, as though in being suspended in this cosmic movement and losing the motility that comes from taking a stand and taking hold, I had found what I went down in the sea to find.

When the sky was red, the sun rolling on the swells, we put our gear again in the boat and headed out to sea. Some seven miles out the sky was indigo and we dropped anchor. We buckled on our breathing apparatus, and dropped into the warm black waves. The sea-lantern pushed out a tube of light in the black, and I hung suspended on it. From time to time the pale form of a fish that had faded out its colors for the night was caught; after a moment the fish awoke and whipped out of the luminous tube which then could not find it again. I turned the lantern down; at the bottom the spiney urchins had come out of their crevices in the reef and were bristling their way across the sea floor, and the moray eels ambled between them. I turned off the light and dissolved into the warm thick dark, hearing it clamp the stream of gases from my lungs into sealed bubbles. The sea was so full of darkness, a space become substance so substantial there could no longer be parts exposed outside of parts or open dimensions. The span of my arms extended a right and a left, but these went no further than the terminations of my own limbs. When I waved my hand the bioluminescent plankton sparkled and died away, without having situated me or them in the lengths and breadths of the oceanic night. Then my hands broke the surface, and I was astonished to know that I had been rising. I redescended and almost at once lost the axis of verticality; I was only in depth. Depth without orientation, without planes or horizons, where nothing approached, nothing receded, no sites held fixed, no distances gauged. Had I descended two or three hundred feet, I would have known the forbidden pressures, but the depth could have been no more absolute.

When the pull of breathing, become harder, indicated my tank was near empty, I forced a mouthful of air into the buoyancy compensator and surfaced. In the black air above the night reigned sovereign, with no moon or clouds. I saw the Milky Way spread across the rolling sea, and the stars glittering among the bioluminescent plankton. It was hard to decide, by approximation, which stars in the distance were the light bubbles of the terra firma in which men stand erect.

The spinning planet had turned its ocean again to the day; I sank through nets of light the equatorial sun suspended now in the deep.

The links of light in the blue spaces illuminate nothing, do not outline or form; they delight. The coral cliffs shiver with millions of antennae. Fish materialize in stripes and streams of color. One sees no bulging stomachs, no lines of force of muscle systems; their shapes are phosphorescent diagrams of gliding among the ceaseless waving of the gorgonians and the trembling tentacles of anemones. At the bottom are stretched the purls and ribs of the fabric nimble laps of the tide are contriving out of white crumbs of the skeletons the coral flowers grew. Unrendable sanctuary veil over the adamantine core, trapped raging lava, or absolute darkness of the depths. Colors spread over the animals of the land and the sky delineate something of the inner organs, and their external forms are informative; colors of the rocks found on dry land reveal the grain or granular inner composition. The deep is all in surface effects. The rapture of the deep is not different from the delight before the fugitive inventions in foam and spray of the waves at the surface.

Yet why must it be that men always seek out the depths, the abyss? Why must thought, like a plumb line, concern itself exclusively with vertical descent? Why was it not feasible for thought to change direction and climb vertically up, ever up, towards the surface? Why should the area of the skin, which guarantees a human being's existence in space, be most despised and left to the tender mercies of the senses? I could not understand the laws governing the motion of thought—the way it was liable to get stuck in unseen chasms whenever it set out to go deep; or, whenever it aimed at the heights, to soar away into boundless and equally invisible heavens, leaving the corporeal form undeservedly neglected.

If the law of thought is that it should search out profundity, whether it extends upwards or downwards, then it seemed excessively illogical to me that men should not discover depths of a kind on the "surface," that vital borderline that endorses our separateness and our form, dividing our exterior from our interior. Why should they not be attracted by the profundity of the surface itself?[2]

Researchers do try to understand the patterns and colors that cover the fish functionally, as camouflage, as when jackfish seen from above are somber blue, merging into the color of the deep, and seen from below are whitish, merging into the color of the light above. Patterns that do not merge with the shapes and tones of the environment can be taken to serve for identifcation among members of the species. Colors and designs that are extreme in contrast with the environment and flauntingly ostentatious are protective, Konrad Lorenz proposed, by virtue of their very aggressivity. In this way our vision in the deep could become profound, penetrating; one would in seeing the color and patterns of the skin comprehend the fish in its functional relationship with species it devours and those that devour it, or comprehend the relationship of recognition with those it does not devour, its species-fellows, or comprehend its expressive-aggressive index. What is not cryptic is semantic, what is not camouflage is anti-camouflage, identification badge and provocation. The logic is impeccable, and holds the mind in the exhaustiveness of its alternative. But does it explain the lengths to which they go—the most flamboyant colors, the most intricate patterns, as though their combat fatigues had been, between one Ice-Age season and the next, redesigned by Milanese haut-couturists with minds empty of everything but frivolity?

Portman introduced the idea of "organs to be looked at."[3] Before the plumage and display behaviors of the bird-of-paradise, before the coiled horns of the mountain sheep, one has to admit a specific development of the organism to capture another eye. The exterior does not only function cryptically to conceal the inner functions, or semantically to attract a fellow of the species to the reproductive organs; it is not enough to relate the exterior functionally to the inner essence. In addition "the eye and what is to be looked at form a functional unity which is fitted together according to rules as strict as those obtaining between food and digestive organs."[4] The symmetry of patterns and the colors have to receive a specific explanation on the level of the phenomenal and not of the operational; there is a logic of ostentation over and beyond camouflage and semantic functions. The color-blind *octopus vulgaris* controls with twenty nervous systems the two to three million chromatophores, iridophores and leucophores fitted in its skin; only fifteen of these have been correlated with camouflage or emotional states. At rest in its lair, its skin invents continuous light shows. The sparked and streaked coral fish school and scatter as a surge of life dominated by a compulsion for exhibition, spectacle, parade. The eye adrift in the deep finds itself in a cosmos of phenomena and not of noumena, a theatrics and not a teleological engineering, a depth of *doxa,* opinion or glory, and not of truth and dissimulation.

Glory is for its witness, the spectacle is for the spectator, the screen of phenomenal effects produced in reality are for a sphere of lucidity, an eye, a mind! With this inference one makes even the gloss of appearance intelligible, and one posits oneself as an essential and necessary factor in the sphere which one enters. One appropriates even this film of semblance and this vanity of appearances. *Omnia ad maiorem gloriam deo*—God himself was said to have been obliged to create man to receive the splendor of his glory.

How derisible is this appropriation! The sailfish, zinging by, sends a flash of iridescence into the water of your eye; who could tell or remember it? When you capture a fish to look at it in your own dry domain, the colors cloud over at once under the sun that illuminates them for you. Even the marbled cowries and the garish crabs, no longer waxed with their life but with shellac, show you but plastic-rose colors. The most artfully blended pigments the deep has to show are inside the shells of the abelones, inside the bones of the parrotfish, on the backs of the living cones, where the very abelones and parrotfish and cones themselves shall never see them. The most ornate skins are on the nudibranchia, blind sea slugs. In the marine abysses, five or six miles below the last blue rays of the light, the fish and the crabs, almost all of them blind, illuminate their lustrous colors with their own bioluminescence, for no witness.

I can then think that I am the eye all this spectacle was inventing itself for in the depths, in the dark, for millions of years. Or, only an eye, a touch, I drift completely a stranger profaning a sphere of resplendent phenomena whose glory, utterly disinterested, calls for no acolyte.

Denuded of one's very postural schema, of one's own motility, swept away and scattered by the surge, one does nothing in the deep. One takes nothing, apprehends nothing, comprehends nothing. One is only a brief visitor, an eye that no longer pilots or estimates, that moves, or rather is moved, with nothing in view.

For the eye moved by the thalassa complex the deep is an erotogenic zone.[5] The eye adrift in the deep is not penetrating, examining, interrogating, surveying, gauging. It passes over surface effects, caresses.

The caress that passes over the surface abdicates its force, it makes contact only to expose itself. It has no ends in mind, is not manipulating means, does not know what it wants. The organ that caresses does not take up or take over, does not appropriate. It returns without return, without profit. The organism that caresses is not gathering sensations, gathering information, perceiving, is not a sense organ. It does not circumscribe forms, is not informed by what it fondles.

Under the caress the substance and the life become skin. With a nudity that is not functional, like that of the bared arms of the laborer, that is not informative, like that of the exposed face and hands of the speaker, that is not graceful, like that of the limbs of the dancer. Under the caress skin extends a wanton and exhibitionist nakedness. It exposes its exorbitant materiality, unformed, uninformative, inoperative, inexpressive, provocative and teasing. Its ardent opaqueness weighs on the arms that embace, afflicts the mobility of organs that touch.

The organs that caress are not being operated by an ego, for its intents and purposes, they are not forcing their movements into receptor substances; they are moved by the movements they provoke in the other. They are agitated by the ripples of aching pleasure that surface in the nakedness they touch, by the torments in the divergences of extension, in the departures of time.

The organ that carresses is afflicted with the passivity and the passion of skin; it is moved, affected, affectionate, moves to be in contact with it, as though in pity, but in a pity that does not know how to console and does not aim to heal, complacent compassion. Forms tremble and deform in the agitations of caresses; gropings, manipulations and abandon succeed one another. The organ that caresses is solicitous, but with an audacious and violent tenderness. It struggles to disrobe, disarm, unmask, denude every decency, to hold every gesture and silence every signal, to disconnect the underlying apparatus, to expose exposure itself. It violates every secrecy without learning anything; it profanes. Profanation designates the violence of the one that breaks into the sacred precincts, the *templum,* that forces the tabernacle where the secret, the wisdom and the law, abide, without discovering anything, finding himself in the presence of the utterly strange, the god.

The eye adrift in the impermanence caresses, is caressed by the laps of brine, the magnesium networks of light, the evanescent slidings of the fish; it is not comprehensive, sagacious or penetrating. It is not seeking to grasp the one behind the diversity, the foundation beneath the attributes, the substrate beneath the surface effects. The eye no longer steers or is stayed by a posture that upholds itself, takes hold, lodges itself. In the deep one is irremediably a visitor, in the alien and estranged from oneself, an eye dismembered and lost, that has no look of one's own.

The imperative to go down into the deep, the thalassa complex, is undoubtedly futile—the deep is not the way to the profound or the substantial—and regressive. One descends to forms of life arrested at stages evolution had taken the mammals, amphibians, reptiles millions of years ago, to forms of life that are part-organs, gone no further than skin, ovaries, or a piece of intestine, or some muscles. One drifts among dismembered partial attempts or rough drafts of evolution, gastrulas, sponges, sea slugs, plume worms, among dwarfish and monstrous forms, boxfish, giant squid; one drifts among them reduced to being part-organ oneself, eye without a look of one's own, touch apprehending, appropriating nothing.

On the coral cliffs there were huge and glamorous eyelashes, jet black but also all the eye-shadow colors, violet, ochre, green, vermillion, that suddenly blinked as one passed, crinoids, eyeless animals consisting of eyelashes and the lids to blink them. There were sea anemones consisting of skin with a single orifice which is simultaneously mouth, anus, and womb, without ganglions, tubes or nerves inside, only a clot of algae growing in the stagnant pool this skin holds. One could think that this skin and these algae form one organism, since not only could the anemone not assimilate any nutrition without the chemical changes the algae produce, but the algae are of a species that has long ago lost the ability to survive anywhere in the sea but inside the tide pools of the anemone's skin. (I, too, eighty percent water of the saline and mineral composition of sea water, am a pail of ocean brine with about as loose a hylomorphic unity of the ingredients!) There were also basket starfish; by day they lumped upon the rock, but at night they unfold into huge and complicated masses of nervous fibers which undulate and shudder fitfully in the water: a whole living being that consists of a bundle of nerves. There were clams that consisted of rose-pink lascivious lips fastened to the alien skeletons of coral colonies. There were animals that consisted in a lock of hair, unfurling in the ocean like some lost memory of mad Ophelia. There were hollow jewels inhabited by big blind animals without sense organs or differentiated limbs, nothing but stomach and muscle. There were medusas pumping, hearts without torsos, whose veins and arteries sucked in the sea. Sea cucumbers look like big bloated caterpillars, but they lay sprawled as they are turned, for the only muscles they have are intestines. The sea was full of the detached organs of some dismembered monster that never was.

Without a posture for holding myself upright, without that inner diagram for holding myself together and appropriating the detachable things outside, organs separated in me too, skin that made contact with the anemone, eyes still full of marine water making contact with the eye stuck on the ganglions of the octopus. A sponge put in a blender and reduced to broth, and then poured into an aquarium, will reassemble itself after a few days; in an hour, on the beach, my inner ingredients, or most of them, would reassemble themselves into that aleatory clustering I call my psychophysical integrity. Like the algae in the sea anemones the bacteria and enzymes that drift in the thermoclimes and currents in my tubes and that I call "me" are perhaps animals only looking after themselves and parasitic on me. There are plankton and krill, sponges and gorgonians within. There are tadpoles and eels by the millions, swimming in the testicles. There are animals occupied with secreting the ribs and the vertebrae, the inner coral reefs.

When one descends into the deep, regresses to the depths, the eye detached from the grasping hand, the mobilizing posture, is detached from its look, moved now by its own voluptuous desire. The voluptuous eye does not seek to comprehend the unity in the surface dispersion of shapes, to penetrate to the substance beneath the chromatic appearances, to comprehensively apprise itself of the functions and the relationships; it caresses, is caressed by the surface effects of an alien domain. It is seeking the invisible. The invisible that the eroticized eye seeks is no longer the substances, the principles, the causes of the alien; it is the alien look.

There is a look, but it does not stay with the eye and does not find the eye again. The look flees into exteriority, into the alien, looks for the other. And the voluptuous eye, that finds it does not have a look of one's own, is seeking in the other for a look, the look of the other.

Paintings are made as snares for the eye.[6] The snare is made of spots of clay and oil on canvas, but the captivated eye seeks the invisible there. It is not, however, seeking for the contours and the colors of Mount Ste.-Victoire; it is seeking Cézanne's look, which escaped from his eye into exteriority a hundred years ago. But when one climbs the real Mount Ste.-Victoire, for the view, one is also not looking for the visual data that fall on the eye as one climbs up the path through the trees. One is seeking the view from the cliffs, from those pine trees up there upon the valley, the look the mountain has.

Voluptuousness becomes passion when one finds one's own eyes captured in the look that has sought one out, finds one's eyes steeped in the frenzy of the lover's gaze.

Knowledge of sharks is accumulated in laboratories, on dissecting tables. Or, a tracking apparatus fixed on its back with a gun, the shark's movements in the open seas are charted by radar and sonar. Its migrations are known by recording the place where one day it is killed, and the numbered band mailed back to the oceanographic institute. Alone in a small boat under the full moon, watching the sharks coming in across the white sands below to feed in the estuary, one knows the form and spring of their boneless cartilaginous bodies with another knowledge. The incontrovertible ugliness of the shark on the laboratory table or in the tank is not the perfect beauty of this shadowy arabesque under the breakers. One knows with a kind of fearful awe, knows with what one labels an emotion seated in fact not in the mind but in one's own tendons and cartilage invented 340 million years ago by the sea which then became the dominion of the shark. As it was the emotion generated in one's own ganglions that, in the fascination, made contact across the most remote distances of evolution with the tentacles of the octopus.[7] So biologically perfect the shark underwent almost no changes in its body as it watched four Ice Ages destroy thousands of species in the oceans and finally left some species alive on dry land. The day one became a diver is the day one encountered the shark, in its domain. The thalassa complex, Ferenczi wrote, repeats the danger of death which our animal ancestors victoriously overcame in the geological cataclysms of the drying up of the sea. The one who longs to descend, himself, into the realm of the shark has known the fearful awe that watched the sharks moving in the layer of moonlit sea beneath him; he is seeking the terror that measures the shape and the size of its power, the stupor that knows what its watery speeds mean to the one its look has sought out, seeking to know what it means to find one's eyes steeped in the despotism of its look. Aristotle defines fear as *lupē tis ē tarachē* "a kind of depression or bewilderment." Fear, Heidegger wrote, is inauthentifying, disperses out of reach whatever powers are one's own, detaches one from a being that is one's own, disintegrates. The one that goes down to the deep goes for the fear.

Off Hikkaduwa, the wreck was sprawled out at 120 feet. There was no way of determining, by looking at these scattered ribs encrusted with spiney urchins, what dock had once built it and what flag it once flew. The fisherman Thilak, half-Malay half-Sinhalese, had known how to find it, but knew nothing of how long it had lain there, or whose eyes those pearls were, whose bones that coral. In the iron caves of its hull black coral grew like ferns, scorpionfish and stingrays waited in the soft white sands the sea scattered, picked up, scattered, over its floors. Looking up, there was the shark. A white-tip, poised like a torpedo circling the ship it had exploded. It turned slightly, its color and contour vanished, and the eye that had been on the lookout was detached from its look, from the seas, caressed by the cold look of the monster.

Notes

1. Sandor Ferenczi, *Thalassa, A Theory of Genitality*, trans. Henry Alden Bunker (New York: Norton, 1968), pp. 18, 49.
2. Yukio Mishima, *Sun and Steel*, trans. John Bester (New York: Grove, 1970), pp. 22-23.
3. Adolf Portman, *Animal Forms and Patterns*, trans. Hella Czech (New York: Schocken, 1967), chap. VI.
4. Ibid., p. 113.
5. "In scopophilia and exhibitionism the eye corresponds to an erotogenic zone; while in the case of those components of the sexual instinct which involve pain and cruelty the same role is assumed by the skin—the skin, which in particular parts of the body has become differentiated into sense organs or modified into mucous membrane, and is thus the erotogenic zone *par excellence*." Sigmund Freud, *Three Essays on the Theory of Sexuality*, trans. James Strachey, The Standard Edition, Vol. VII (London: Hogarth, 1953), p. 169.

6. Jacques Lacan, *The Four Fundamental Concepts of Psychoanalysis*, trans. Allen Sheridan (New York & London: Norton, 1981), p. 101.

7. "I think that if you asked any zoologist to select the single most startling feature in the whole animal kingdom, the chances are he would say, not the human eye, which by any account is an organ amazing beyond belief, not the squid-octopus eye, but the fact that these two eyes, man's and squid's, are alike in almost every detail." N. J. Berrill.

Savages

"DECEMBER 20. WITH THE CAR N's COUSIN HAD LENT ME, I SET out for Keekorok. I had been driving in some track for two hours, taking this or that branch when it forked without system or clew, quite lost. Then in the pathless grass there was a Maasai woman, waving her hand up and down. I stopped, she got in, carefully arranging her stick and calabash on the floor of the car. I looked at the map, and pronounced quizzically the names of all the marked encampments, rivers, tribal areas I hoped were in the vicinity. Nothing seemed to draw a response from her. I could not recognize anything in what she jabbered. I started up the car and drove on. She was perhaps about fifty, naked save for a piece of red cloth around her shoulders, covered with a scabby layer of dust. Here all the rivers are infested with biharzia, carried by the water snails, killing you of brain fever if you bathe in them—after years of lethargy and internal decay. Perhaps she, like the Dinka, bathes in the urine flowing directly from her cows. She had a finely chiseled face, with thin aquiline nose, high forehead and completely shaven head, but the nobility that imposed was then broken by the loose rims of her toothless mouth. Her earlobes had been perforated with big holes on top, in which the yellow teeth of animals, maybe jackels or warthog piglets, had been inserted; the bottoms had been elongated, and hung now like fat rubber bands. They had been weighted with metal chunks, and decorated with flimsy baskets of beaded threads. Her flat breasts hung down like gloves over the tight folds of her lean stomach. Her lower abdomen and thighs had been scarified and were covered with regular rows of warts. She smiled ingenuously whenever there was any kind of event along the track, and occasionally let out streams of talk ending with a strange prolonged syllable, something like "eeyhh," sing-song, each time on a different pitch. We drove through the length of the afternoon, for four hours, under the bleached out vagueness of the sky. On all sides the savanna continued, without contours or dimensions. Yet in this region Leakey and his archaeologists had dug up *homo habilis* from four million years ago. Everywhere in the same density the termite hills, five or six feet high built up in flabby tubes of the earth color of dried blood. They, unlike Maasai huts made from cow dung, last beyond one rainy season. Everywhere the thorn trees, thinly spaced and malignant in the dust. From time to time in the distance dark specks trembled in the strata of heat: herds of wildebeest, or zebras. The Maasai woman would murmur at the sight of them, waving her hands in appreciation. From time to time in the gullies along the track, or in the gullies the track became, there were two or three hyenas that loped off cringing and low-rumped into the bush. Twice there was an elephant, at a great distance, alone, dried-blood red too with the earth that coated it, and then the whole landscape seemed antedeluvian and monstrous to me.

"Then abruptly the Maasai woman began pointing down and signaling. I understood she wanted me to stop. I looked about: there was nothing whatever to be seen but the vague and interminable savanna, the termite hills and the thorn trees. She carefully gathered up her stick and calabash, got out of the car and pronounced something brief, a formula probably, with an utterly inexpressive, even terribly remote face. Then she began walking off. I could see nothing, no path, nothing that might serve as any kind of landmark. I drove up to the top of the rise, then got out and stood on the bumper of the car; still nothing to be seen before her. I watched her until she had finally dissolved in the vibrating horizon."

What is this thing about savages? On the part of a professor who should be writing abstracts on semiotics and counterfactual conditionals for the state university? On the part of this German woman? Why did she, at the age of seventy-three, leave the white comfort and competence of Germany, and the brawny, Olympian health of Germans, to go look for savages?

Well, it's sex, isn't it? She says it, doesn't she, Leni Riefenstahl explaining her expedition to Kau:

> But oh! the sight that greeted us! Were these 'my' Nuba? I found it hard to grasp the change that had overtaken them. Their cheerful expressions had vanished and their bodies were hideously attired in darned and ragged clothing. Gone, too, was the bead jewelery with which they had once adorned themselves. A whole world collapsed in ruins, but I strove to conceal my disappointment rather than betray how distressed I was by their appearance... We showed the Nuba my book and saw them look ashamed of their erstwhile nakedness. The age of paradisal innocence was dead....
>
> Shortly before our departure—we spent only four weeks with our Nuba—I had a dream. I saw two black men fighting with curved blades attached to their wrists. Moving with almost balletic grace, each of them skillfully evaded the other's onslaughts. Then I saw blood—a lot of it. At that moment I woke up... But the dream-images had rekindled my desire to track down the knife-fighting Nuba.[1]

In *Vanishing Africa*[2] Mirella Ricciardi reveals how she was arrested and almost expelled from Kenya after the Maasai, who at first welcomed her fully, gradually came to think her interest in photographing the nakedness of their young men was pornographic. When she managed, through connections in high government ministries, to get back to them, she found it advisable not to photograph young men head-on. And now we find that the Maasai section of her book begins with four close-ups of the bare behinds of warriors.

"Then I saw blood—a lot of it." Not exactly the sort of libido that warms up to *Kirche, Küche und Kindern*. Savages—that means: sex and cruelty.

They are naked—without clothes or morality. And they are nameless—without ego, personality or individuality. In Bali the first child born, whether it be boy or girl, is called Wayan. The second is Madé, the third Nyoman, and fourth Ktut. With the fifth, they start the series over again. First, Second, Third, Fourth, First, Second. . . It is true that on the child's first birthday, there is a ceremony in which the *pemangku* writes down on leaves several auspicious names, fished out of the stock by divination, then burns the leaves. Whatever name might still be legible in the ashes is assigned to the child. But it is a sacred, and secret, name, and after a few years even the father has forgotten what it was. The child's family and playmates will no doubt tag him with some derisive nickname, as with kids everywhere. The photographs we look at are always just labeled "A Maasai moran," "A Samburu woman." This namelessness is part of our relationship with savages—just as those who love pre-renaissance painting or medieval cathedral sculpture cite its anonymousness as an index of its spirituality. Although Willet, in his book *African Art,* does assert that in Nigeria or in Guinea a man can get a whole personality cult going with his carvings, and that the reason they are all anonymous, or identified as "Benin carving, 19th c.," or "Central Togoland, early 20th c." by those whose vocation and passion is to record, catalogue and label, to museum-ify is that the connoisseur who collected this mask or this fetish couldn't pronounce or remember such "names."

Of all that is savage about savages, the most savage is what they do to themselves. They paint, puncture, tattoo, scarify, cicatrize, circumcise, subincise themselves. They use their own flesh as so much material at hand for—what? We hardly know how to characterize it—Art? Inscription? Sign-language? Or isn't all that more like hex signs? Aren't they treating themselves like the pieces of dikdik fur, bat's penis, warthog's tooth, hornbill bird's skull they attach to themselves? All that excites some dark dregs of lechery and cruelty in us, holding our eyes fixed with repugnance and lust. Otherwise, a naked savage would be no more interesting than the baboons, sticking out their bare asses and genitalia as they scramble along, or the orangutans, with their thin hair that doesn't soften or adorn and thus really doesn't cover over their gross bodyness.

The Mayas inserted the soft skull of a baby into a wooden mold at birth, which flattened back the forehead and pushed the brain cavity out at the sides. They hung a stone in front of the baby's brow, so that it would become somewhat cross-eyed, a characteristic they found attractive. They perforated the earlobes, nostrils, lower lip, to insert wires, teeth of animals, beads, chains, rings. They filed the teeth, and inserted inlays of stone or obsidian into them. They clitoridectomized the girls and circumcised the boys, tattooed the penis and inserted pieces of bone and colored stone and rings into the flesh of the glans. They scarified the plane surfaces of the body, abdomen, breasts, buttocks, such that welts and raised warts covered them, in rows and patterns. They left their fingernails and toenails grow into foot-long, twisting, useless claws. They pierced the nipples, and inserted rings in them. In most of Africa circumcision and clitoridectomy—this inordinate involvement of the public in one's private parts, this cutting into the zone of the most sensitive pleasure nerves and glands—is in fact the main ceremony; most of the songs, dances and instrumental playing the tourist who demands and pays for the maintenance of indigenous cultural forms in the neocapitalist African nations of today hears and sees are in fact songs about circumcision and clitoridectomy, dances these bizarre operations excite in the encampments in the bush.

What we are dealing with is inscription. Where writing, graphics, is not inscription on clay tablets, bark or papyrus, but in flesh and blood, and also where it is not historical, narrative. Where it is not significant, not a matter of marks whose role is to signify, to efface themselves before the meaning, or ideality, or logos. For here the signs count: they *hurt*. Before they make sense to the reader, they give pain to the living substrate. Who can doubt, after Nietzsche, after Kafka (*On the Genealogy of Morals II, The Penal Colony*) that before they informed the understanding of the public, this pain gave pleasure to its eyes?

Inscription, then, writing, does not simply originate from care for and respect for oral speech. Plato's innocence can no longer be ours—Plato who took writing to be a copy of a copy, visual imitation of the phonic stream of vocal signs, which is itself a copy or imitation of the logos, the chain of ideas. Significant writing, historicizing writing, begins with empires; it is invented to inscribe the decrees, the *ipsissima verba* of the despot. Then it is lined up with oral language, becomes subordinate to it, making possible its reproduction.

It is not that savages do not know graphics and inscription, or had not yet come to use clay or papyrus instead of their own skin as the inscribed surface. After all, despots branded their decrees on their subjects as well as on their monuments. But before historical—narrative, signifying, phonocentric, logocentric—inscription, there is a savage inscription not yet despotic, not serving oral speech. It pains, rather than signifies. Not only during the supremely public moment of the inscription itself. Each time the clitoridectomized woman copulates, the stiff penis in her rasps her with her scarred labia. One can understand that it is not only their narrow pelvis that makes the Bantu women eat little and water down the milk they drink during pregnancy so that the delivery will not be too difficult!

And yet are not all these scarifications, perforations, incisions bound up somehow with the exorbitant pleasure the savage takes in himself? Wretch as that Maasai moran may look, his elongated earlobes and perforated nostrils stripped now of their beads and animals' fangs, his dusty body covered with cheap Hong Kong pants and shirt, still holding on to his stick among the business-suited black banktellers and miniskirted secretaries of Nairobi, still it is doubtful that there ever was a human culture in which a man thought more highly of himself.

It is the circle of warts raised around the eyes, it is the perforated ears that marks him out for us. It is the inscription and the codification that makes the savage.

His body is used as a surface for inscription of—we hesitate now to say "signs"—marks, marks painful and pleasurable. Anonymous marks, tribal marks. Without clothing to shield it from the dust, it is covered with dirt, and oiled and painted with clay. The body of a savage is so much earth, so much clay, a cuneiform tablet. It is not, as ours for us, the very expression, moment by moment, of an inward spirit, or a person belonging to himself. It loses, or does not yet have status, dignity, while no longer, like that of the baboons and the gibbons, expressing the vital functions of the species. For the tattooed breast is no longer exposed with the contours of a mammary gland; it is but the surface for an inscription that extends up the throat, down the stomach, and draws its own borders around itself.

There is inscription, and there is codification. Operations strange and uncivilized, as well as not natural, not biological. Inscription and codification of what? Of, we shall say, excitations.

For the classical ideas of philosophy shall not be of use to us when we are dealing with savages. Classical philosophy took the life in us to consist in a sort of inward depth, which could be seen exteriorized, expressed, on the articulations of the body. It would consist in processes, sensations, thoughts, volitions. They could be known through their expressions. And one does not know one's own life in a way so very different from the life in another: one sees one's own movements, the tensions that take form in one's positions, one harkens to the words forming in oneself, verbal signs, expressions, of the processes of thought in oneself.

Intentionality is the modern formula for this philosophical classicism. Not only the conscious mind, but—this was the central thesis of existential philosophy—all the processes of life are intentional processes. Something—a physico-chemical, an electrical stimulus, hyletic data—begins to refer to something, to signify something, begins to function as a sign. Then it is a sensation. A sensation is an intentional excitation. Something—a physico-chemical state of the stomach, of the vegetative glandular system—begins to signify something, to aim at something, to tend toward something. It is a desire, want or volition—an intentional state. The life in the corporeal depths consists of such intentional processes. The moves, positions, utterances of the body, these muscular contractions, these physico-chemical phenomena, function intentionally, function to signify something—and we say that that body is alive.

Speech as a corporeal possibility can be immediately understood with this concept. Certain movements, certain muscular contractions, of themselves expressive like all our vital movements and positions, have been conventionalized. What makes it possible for them to be expressive is the intentional processes that animate them, the signifying sensations excited in them, and which are the life in the inner depths of the speaking body.

Well, if one can conventionalize one's vocal utterances and facial movements, if one can intentionally give color and shape and relief to them, if one can codify one's hand movements too, and one's steps, and the thrust of one's chest, then one could also paint and mold them, make an ideogram of one's earlobes or one's penis. Would we not thus have comprised all this tattooing, perforating, cicatrizing, clitoridectomizing within the classical theory of intentionality and of life?

Yet—there subsists the feeling that the savages are going too far. But could there be anything objectionable in extending expression, intentionality, life? Yet—the theory does not make us understand the repugnance we feel, over the indecency of it all, the savagery of it all.

In *Beyond the Pleasure Principle* Freud was working at a concept of the libidinal essence of life. He did not begin with the concept of intentions, or of sensations, that is, signifying impressions; he worked with the concept of excitations. The Freudian distinction between primary processes and secondary processes is not a distinction between sensations, intentional processes, and the pure excitations that would have been their raw material. It is rather a distinction between freely mobile excitations and bound excitations.

The term *excitation* is not a physico-chemical term; an excitation is not the simple effect of a stimulus, a transmission of energy. It occurs in the physico-chemical mass of material nature when there is an effect disproportionate to its cause. These effects are libidinal life itself. Their nature can be circumscribed, at least, with the terms intensity and discharge, pain and pleasure, putting together these two sets of concepts, physical and psychic. They are moments when force intensifies, when a surplus builds in the machinery, when a potential upsurges, a superabundance, that then discharges. The release of this force, its dying, is felt as pleasure.

We have to think of this vital effervescence, this layer of libidinal life, as a sheer multiplicity of these effects, these excitations. It is not their nature to coagulate into one, or be all commanded from one central instance. It is not their movement to stabilize, to fix themselves, to tend to a state of contentment, full content, and then maintain that. In them pain and pleasure are phases of one impulse, and life and death inextricable.

This libidinal life should not be pictured, topographically, as a depth of inward life. It is superficial, all surface. It is the slippery effervescence at the conjuncture of mouth with breast, anus and exterior, urethra at the point where the urine surfaces, thumb with lips, finger with nostril. Couplings, for the sake of the surface effects—that is the machinery of the libido. The libidinal zone in the body is the skin—skin and the mucous orifices that prolong it inward, but where the finger, tongue or penis will make contact with more skin.

There is something artificial about saying that the libidinal excitations occur on the skin—as though we already had a non-libidinal view of our bodies and of the membrane covering them. For through the free excitations which intensify and discharge, a body-surface first extends. We should say that the excitations, in their ephemeral and passing multiplicity, distend a zone which is all surface. Their movement is very different from the intentional movements of classical philosophy. Those exist by extending themselves, by moving, from hyletic datum to its meaning, from the material sensation to its sense or signified referent, from the immanent, inward zone where life is excited to the exterior, objective sphere of the outlying world. The movement of the primary process, of the libidinal excitations, is horizontal, from one contact-point on the skin to another. Even when one enters into the orifices that open on the body surface, the finger, tongue or penis that penetrates does not make contact with a sphere of immanence, a control-room or broadcasting studio; it only slides in into more surface effects. Wet pants, pap slobbered over one's chest and thighs, what difference, for the finger that plays with that, from the saliva in one's mouth, the poo in one's anus? Wet inner surface of the lip dragged over the shoulders, ejaculating penis rolling over her breasts, labia rubbing over his nose, two lovers are sea cucumbers turning their organs inside out, as sluggish.

Life reduced to the coupling of mouth with breast, and the slobber, and the gurgling, the surface effects. Finally the tubes are all full, the body a sack of milk, blood, and urine. The eyes close, the fingers break contact, the thumb plugs up the mouth. The soft vesicle closes up. It rejects, repels with peevish movements the breast offered still, the maternal lips that want to kiss back their reward for generosity. Irritated by all that. Not interested in saying anything, in saying thanks. Not anxious about death. Just wants to curl up, to shut the eyes, plug the ears, seal the orifices, a body without organs, as Deleuze and Guattari,[3] and Artaud, say. Nothing but a closed, full corpuscle, cell filled with milk and blood and soft ooze shit. Sleep. Unconscious. Id.

What is the relationship between this body without organs and those excitations, those couplings? It is hard to think of them as in a relationship of cause and effect, or intentionality and expression. The libidinal surface is not teleproduced by the full body, which rather repels it. It is not the surface *of* this depth, in the sense that, in the intentional perspective, the mobile face is the surface of the soul. The libidinal skin is not part of the functional machinery of the body, like the fenders, gear housing and windshield of a motorcycle. It does not protect the inner body; it irritates it. The libidinal surface does not open into the closed plenum. Through all its orifices the libidinal excitations only travel along more surfaces; the libidinal surface is a Möbius strip.

We would lose again the sense of the erotogenic surface and of the closed body without organs if we tried to conceive of their relationship classically, in terms of hylomorphism or functionalism. We should not look for an intentional arc or postural schema that would make of this full and whole body without organs the integrating causality or finality of the parts, the surface couplings. The surface effects do not emanate out of the depth of the full body; rather they occur at the couplings where buzzing, slobbering lips, where tingling nipples, where toes and soft soles of feet make contact with the milk foam, the rough goatskin blanket, the hairy blades of grass. And they do not feed into the body core: the buzzing lips prolong their own vibrations without expressing anything or ingesting anything, the hands disconnect from the posture and wallow about, spreading the tickling across the flaccid surfaces of limbs. Pleasures of the blinking eyelids in a tingling field of sweating pores, flicked ears, nasal hairs quivering and sneezy.

The body plenum, closing in on itself, repels all these excitations, these irritations. At the same time it attracts them. The membrane with which it has wrapped up all its inner soft flows and secretions functions as a smooth surface across which the excitations slide. On it occur couplings, where gelatinous organisms—eyes, waxy ear tubes, saliva glands, sweat buds, musc glands—lap on to the extraneous flows of useless sunlight, pepper and kelp, wooly fibers, squirming microorganisms—like sea anemones attached to the reef and lapping at the marine sludge with their amorphous tubes, through which it drains on without being held long enough to ripple the surf. But a spasm in any one of these touchy masses of tentacles spreads across the whole colony. Thus the membrane with which the inner body closes itself up in itself also serves as a surface upon which all the libidinal couplings are attached, unstably, across which they are distributed, across which their susceptibilities send their shiverings and squalls. It is by virtue of its closure, its smoothness, that they are freely mobile. And connect up, in turbulent ways, an excitation here not following one fixed afferent path, jumping over synapses, taking both paths at a fork, coupling up laterally, as when two sea anemones get tangled in one another with all their Medusa hair.

These circuits of excitation fall back on themselves. They intensify, vibrate on themselves, are consumed. They do not emanate out of, nor get sent into, a central subsistent identity, an immanent ego; they are not predicates of the being that is one and selfsame by being invariably for-itself. The excitation intensifies, is supported by its own substance, and explodes into itself. Forming the incandescence of a reflection, an ipseity. This ipseity is not produced by a mirror-effect. It is produced by an intensity affected with itself, a pleasure tormented by itself, a torment complacent in itself, voluptuous, a lust luxuriating in itself. The subjectivities are multiple, unpredictable, ephemeral. Peripheral egoisms—surface effects. A mouth that found a breast—that makes an egoism. A finger that found an orifice. A drop of starlight, after traveling a billion lightyears through void, lapped up by the jelly of an eye. A womb into which, this hot Benares evening, flow the waters of the Ganges, coming from the naked body of Shiva in his icy Himalayan lair. The ashes into which innumerable Hindus have been disintegrated collecting on the vaginal slime. The black testicles tingling against the pelt of a lion, this equatorial high noon in Ethiopia, when all the savanna is vibrating. The identities that take form in these couplings do not have names in our nomenclature of I, you, Tom, Dick, Mary, Creon, Jocasta, Oedipus. We should have to invent new names—Starlight-Lips, Boneash-Clitoris, Lionpelt-Testicles, Flibbertigibbet-Tongue. Buggering Thunderbolt, Hymen-ripping Holy Ghost.

But how, you ask, could one name, how identify, these flickering subjectivities, these voodoo personalities? Are not all these surface egos but so many witchdoctor masks, without juridical personality? Would we not make ourselves ridiculous by trying to name these simulacra of subjective identity, these savage egos utterly irresponsible which one can call up but not count on? No doubt. And yet, inconsistent as they are, these nodes in the erotogenic zone, these subjects of pleasure and torment, communicate among themselves, have some kind of identity by bricolage, made of the dismembered limbs of savages, beasts, stars, demons, the debris thrown outside of civilization, heaped up if not synthesized, and some kind of incandescence in their conflagration. And they do communicate, among themselves, hyenas laughing on the surface of the night. How? How can such subjectivity, insubstantial and ephemeral, a subjectivity by collage rather than by synthesis, communicate with another, that is, excite, tease, provoke, arouse another? How, indeed, does *any* subjectivity communicate?

The smooth, closed membrane of the full and whole body without organs forms the surface upon which these couplings are attached, which they irritate, where they are distributed, where they elaborate their linkages, upon which these peripheral egos, these voluptuous subjectivities proliferate to consume the surplus potential the full body without organs refuses. Underneath there is this closed vesicle, circulating its vague and undifferentiated flows, torpid and sterile. But it would be a mistake to think of this contentment as an integrity, an aboriginal synthesis, a transcendental apperception. There is not an I at some nerve-center of all that material, there is only Id. There is not some incomparable individuality that possesses its own formula, and elaborates itself. Here what misleads us is our arithmetic. We hoist up the baby up out of the mess all over the floor, we pull the savage out of the bush, focus the range-finder and the f-stop, point to the area within the contours, and say: that is a unit! $1 = I$.

In reality the body without organs constitutes itself by ingestion, introjection. It is a born cannibal; on the Day of Judgment, Saint Thomas Aquinas wondered, by what epistemological processes, beyond all human understanding, will God know who gets the body? Whose blood is this, whose milk? Come on, fill up, Snooks: one teaspoon for mummy, one for daddy, one for baby. The full body constitutes itself by incorporation and not by internal self-synthesis. How good it feels to be full of shit. Whose shit is this, whose dirt? To make the anus a private part is the first move toward the constitution of the private individual, who belongs to himself, and toward private property and capitalism. In fact everybody is interested in baby's poo—mummy and daddy, and baby too, who would just as readily ingest it again if they didn't grab it first. It's all dirt, isn't it? All earth. The earth, the great body of the somnolent planet is one with the baby, with the savage that curls up in the dust or in the caves. The earth is in fact the original body without organs, closed in itself, full and warm, enormous vesicle suspended in the void, stuffed full of its warm flows, gurgling and belching from time to time, sufficiency itself.[4] The undifferentiated closure of the body without organs, coagulation of matter which is flows and dirt, does not have something like personal identity, or logically irreducible individuality; it has tellurian oneness, contentment coagulated out of cannibalism and coprophagy. The membrane that one has photographed and taken to fix the contours of an irreducible hylomorphic individual is in fact vermicular casing—a tube in which everything gets turned into dirt.

Whence the instability characteristic of these subjectivities, these nodes of identity, that form in the erotogenic zone. Are they the subjectivities of this core body, this Id, in the sense that, in the classical body, the soul is the form of the amorphous prime matter of the body? Are they somehow the cause, or at least the finality, of its being a unit? Or is subjectivity transcendental; are they related as transcendental ground is to the empirically conditioned? Or is the ego the function through which the Id enters into relationship with the outside? Answer: none of the above.

The body without organs is closed, forms a unit, but does so by continual introjection and tellurimorphosis. It is one with the eminent, incomparable unity of the earth, a unity by emanation, where one plus one makes one. The coupling of mouth with breast, and the surplus pleasure that occurs, and that is consumed right there in a surface ego formed for that—is that ego attached to the depth body of the infant or of the mother? The coupling of the Maasai's heart with the lion's testicles attached to it by a ring through the perforated nipple—the excitation that occurs there, and the eddy of subjectivity that feeds on that excitement, is it an ego attached to the warrior or attached to the lion? The Samburu curling up in the cave is drawn back into the womb of the earth, and the contentment that simmers there is attached to the full body of the earth. The savage ego is nomadic; take him out of his bush and you have put out all the fires in his eyes, taken all the egoism out of his chest and legs, taken all the conceit out of his dusty prick.

The inscription, then, the graphics? We proposed to distinguish this work savages do on the material of their bodies from making signs, from expression. Moravia distinguishes between what he calls the psychological face, that of the African living in cities, already civilized, and the sculptured face of the African who lives in the bush. Italian bodies are expressive; they make, minute by minute, every part the exterior their bodies present into signs. But they do not scarify, cicatrize, clitoridectomize themselves, like savages. What they do is a work done on the surface layer by which it is made to connect up, not with the glandular secretions, disgestive processes, flows of blood, fermenting gases, bile in the inner functional body, but rather with the intentions in the psychic depth. The surface figures, articulations, moves are made into a zone of systematic mediation between inward, depth intentions and transcendent objects, goals, landscapes of the world beyond. The surface is not laid out for itself; it is completely occupied by signs which simultaneously refract your gaze off into the street, into the horizon, into history where their signified referents are, and open in upon the psychic depth where the intentions are being formed. Whence the transparency of the Italian exterior; the cartilage and opaque, rubbery padding of blind flesh with all its lubricating and irrigating pores thins out: you see by looking at him how an Italian fits into the field of operations of the middle and high bourgeoisie, how he relates to a landscape of renaissance palaces, baroque churches, fascist imperial avenues, you see what he is thinking and what he wants. The way she plucks her eyebrows and he cuts his mustache, the signs she paints across her mouth in phosphorescent paint and the angle at which he braces up his cock in its pouch under his nylon swim trunks—all that has nothing to do with the tattooing and body painting and penis sheaths of savages. All that is civilized, *significant*.

These cicatrizations, these scarifications, these perforations, these incisions on the bodies of savages—they hurt. The eye that looks at them does not read them; it winces, it senses the pain. They are points of high tension; intensities zigzag across them, releasing themselves, dying away orgasmically, into a tingling of pleasure. In voluptuous torments, more exactly, and not in contentment, that is, comatose states of equilibrium. In intensive moments when a surface, surplus potential accumulates, intensifies, and discharges. The savage inscription is a working over the skin, all surface effects. This cutting in orifices and raising tumescences does not contrive new receptor organs for the depth body, nor multiply ever more subtle signs for the psychic depth where personal intentions would be being formed; it extends the erotogenic surface.

Sure, it is a multiplication of mouths, lips, labia, anuses, these sweating and bleeding perforations and puncturings, it is a proliferation of pricks, these scarifications, these warts raised all over the abdomen, around the eyes, these penis heads set with feathers and hair, these heads with hair tressed into feelers, antennae of beady and lascivious insects. The oral and anal phase not overcome, renounced, but deviated, the excitations gone to seed, running everywhere, opening up lips and sphincters all across the weaned body, lunatic like the sea according to Nietzsche, rising up in a million lips to the full moon. The phallic dominion decentralized.

But what does one gain by all that? Isn't it civilized, efficient, to invest everything in your cock, and incorporate everything in your vagina? Isn't all the rest so much stupidity, savagery? What is more unnatural than a savage?

In fact the libidinal zone is perverse from the start, and is constituted in perversity. Freud finds it beginning as soon as life begins—but by a deviation. He does not see it in the sucking and the pleasure of sucking, that is, the contentment of filling up and becoming a full sack of warm fluid. That is no more libidinally productive than the cactus roots drawing in the rain. He sees it in the slobbering, the drooling, in this excess potential left on the surface, and from which the coupling derives a surplus pleasure. It is not the holding in, or the expelling of the shit that makes the dirty baby, it is the smearing it around. That is why, in our analysis, we distinguished two processes, the production of the closed and sterile body without organs, full and contented, and the production of the libidinal excitations, the surface effects.

The white men, electrical engineers and geologists on contract, have their own view of excitations and of the earth. They are Reichians by night, believing in total orgasm; they are, Derrida says, phallocrats. For them the penis is the drive shaft of the inner machinery of the body; it delivers the power. That's how it works. For whitemen know how things work, not like the jerkoffs in the bush. That's the productive attitude, or, more exactly, the reproductive. But isn't that what sex is really about, filling that hole with a man?

The savages don't seem convinced. Freud neither. An erection, it is true, that delivers the baby, but the fun is not in that. Libidinally, an erection extends the surface. And, of course, hardens it, concentrates the tension, for the voluptuous release. Opening up your labia, letting the vaginal fluids run, that of course delivers the egg. But the orgasms extend the surface. When you get laid you get laid out. The Möbius strip coils in on itself, but it is still all surface, inner face or outer face, it is all equivalent. The tensions dance. Ephemeral subjectivities, brief egos, throb and get consumed down there, in the flows.

It is a little discouraging, after all these years, to realize that the problem boils down to that of the one and the many, more exactly, of the nature of the identity involved in subjectivity. The arithmetical solution seemed the simplest, to the Western mind; ascribe everything to a transcendental ego. What one has, in the air-conditioned bedroom, is an entity: a man, a woman. A phallic machine, coupled on to a womb. The subject, to which this complex, but everywhere lined up, operation is predicated, the subject which is affected by it all and contented with it all, is a unit, a transcendent selfsameness. It is behind everything, the information-seat; it is under everything, the support or substrate.

But let us try, now, to see things from the libidinal point of view, where the egos are multiple and superficial, surface effects. They form at the couplings, where an excess potential develops. A mouth, it is adjustable. It can couple on to a nipple—or a bottle, or a thumb. A hand can curl around a breast, or an arm, or another hand, or a penis. An ear is an orifice in which you can insert mother's or lover's babble, or a finger, or a penis, or a cheetah's tooth. A baby in a buggy, a savage in the bush, proceeds by bricolage, and not by blueprint. As long as the inner sack is filled, what does it matter? The body without organs is profoundly indifferent to these surface couplings. No ego still burns in the suffocating morass down in there, in that, Id. The moments of subjectivity, of pleasure tormented with itself, of torment incandescent with itself, are all on the surface.

As a result the egos that form are not necessarily of the male, lack of a vagina, form, and of the female, lack of a penis, form. There are lips sucked out on my thighs—places where the green mamba kissed me, and these incisions that remain, to mark the pain and the pleasure. The couplings multiply, extend the libidinal zone. They leave their marks, so that one can return to them, or, more exactly, so that an egoism can take pleasure at these points where tensions accumulate, can consume that surplus energy. We have to not only fasten our attention on these multiple and unstable erotic identities, which requires a certain discipline so that we do not slide back into our civilized habits of just ascribing everything to some ineffable, transcendental, but simple, selfsame ego activating everything. We also have to try to maintain that strange Neoplatonic logic of identity involved in the Id, in the closed and full vesicle whose membrane is irritated and inscribed by these excitements, which is all closed in itself, inert and sterile, and yet is indistinguishable from dirt, from the closed body of the earth itself—like the One in Plotinus from which emanates another one, which cannot get out of it enough to make two. These cuts and scars on the face of the Yoruba are the claw-marks of Agazu, but they are not just zones of his body destroyed by the totemic leopard, for they are his pleasure and his pride and his very identity. He arises, out of this coupling, as the one that was strong enough to be chosen by, and to hold the embrace of, the leopard. And this identity, this subjectivity, is not just attached to the physiological unit of this Yoruba male, it is attached to the leopard land. What will Social Security identity, by number, add to this identity born in pain and pleasure, voluptuous identity?

It belongs to the nature of graffiti not to pay heed to borders, to spread right over obstacles, to make walls of different angles, doors, openings, all the support of one inscription that pursues itself. The inscription extends the erotogenic surface.

It is also a first codification of desire. Not coding in the sense that the functioning of every machine, of every gene and cell carries its own code, by which the operations effected are internally determined. Codification in the sense of conventionalization, socialization. But this socialization is already oppression, forced from the outside but working within by repression.

We said that these incisions, these welts and raised scars, this graphics, are not signs; they are intensive points. They do not refer to intentions in an inner individual psychic depth, nor to meanings or concepts in some transcendent beyond. They reverberate one another. But they are lined up. Warts and scarifications in rows, in circles, in swasticas, in zigzags.

What is the nature of the system involved? These are, for the most part, not representations. The Japanese art of tattooing pictures of animals, people and landscapes on the body belongs to civilization and not to savagery. But the patterns of marks are also not governed by a logical grammar. We have to fix the level at which inscription is neither representational, pictographic, commanded by sensuous originals, nor alphabetical, made to correspond to phonic originals, nor ideogrammic or logical, corresponding to a conceptual order, to ideal forms. They are, we said, lined up with one another; the duplication is lateral, on the same plane. Penises and fingers, vaginal, oral, and anal orifices repeating themselves. The repetition across time of intensive discharges of which they are the centers gives rise to a repetition of intensive centers across space. But putting it that way is to speak as though we have a time and a space already given a priori, in which the excitations occur, repeating themselves and projecting new sites for themselves. In fact it is the pulse of intensification and discharge that is the first form of a moment in life, and the libidinal impulses first mark out, or temporalize, a time made of moment upon moment. And it is the incision and tumescence of new intensive points, pain-pleasure points, that first extends the erotogenic extension. What we have, then, is a spacing, a distributive system of marks. They form not representations and not signifying chains, but figures, figures of intensive points, whose law of systematic distribution is lateral and immanent, horizontal and not transverse. This Nuba belly is a chessboard or pin-ball machine; there are places marked, fixed, but each place communicates laterally with further places, and the ball you shoot into it can jump in any direction from any place, according to the force with which it spins.

So far we have been envisaging the inscription purely as productive. By its material operation—by the incisions, the scarification—and by its systematic distributive spacing—which proceeds by repetition and divergence—it extends the erotogenic surface, produces a place or a plane productive of pleasurable torments, of voluptuous moments of subjectivity. But these very same intensive points now become demands, appeals. For something, someone, absent. They become marks for-another, they form the gaping cavities of demand, want, desire, hunger. They have not yet become signs—for what they refer to is not something ideal, transcendent meaning, but another intensive point; these scarifications, these raised hardnesses on the pliable flesh call for another's eye, another's touch, finger, nipple, tongue, penis. The reference becomes a lack, and its direction unilateral.

This is not yet a semiotic system. Yet it is out of this kind of distributive movement of inscription that the differentiated material for a semiotic system will be taken, and on this purely lateral and libidinal function of craving and want that the intentional reference of signs will be developed.

What is disturbing is the reversal we find here: an intensive mark, produced by voluptuous pain and productive of pleasurable torments, becomes a point of lack, demand, and craving. But there has not been a dialectical reversal, from potential to craving, from positive to negative. They are both there, in something less than a synthesis. There has occurred a kind of depression, a hollowing out, such that the force and excitation of an intensity, productive of an egoism, a local and intensive subject to consume it, becomes now the force of a craving for another, becomes a demand for, an appeal to another. This depression is the very locus of repression and oppression; here is the vortex where the explosive libidinal excitations are repressed, and where the force of oppression by the social body invests the singular one. Here begins the breeding of the herd animal, a form of life in which every impulse is felt as a want, in which every excitation, every libidinal intensity that produces a moment of subjectivity, appeals to the herd. The ephemeral singularity of subjectivity becomes intrinsically gregarious; the human animal becomes socialized.

Nietzsche wrote that only the least and worst part of our life becomes conscious, that is, gets verbalized, gets put into signs. But the verbalization, the becoming-conscious, is not the operation that makes the forces that have been marked into signs; the inscribed flesh has been significant long before the voice. All our impulses, all our libidinal intensities productive of moments of subjectivity, turn into signs, that is, into wants, demands addressed to another, appeals made to another. A subjectivity completely made of impulses, we become a bundle of needs, of wants, servile animals, consumers. The force of the libidinal charge turns into the sniveling need to be loved. All our productive forces, all the surplus excitation produced on the libidinal surface, only serves to bind us into herds of animals that need one another. The intensive surface of our life is exposed to the public eye, not to the eye that feels and caresses, that is pained and exhilarated, but to the judging eye, the eye that appraises and evaluates, rewards, redeems, and blames, culpabilizes. The eye that makes human animals ashamed of their nakedness.

But these must not be taken as successive operations. There is a kind of inscription that decrees, condemns and punishes—all at once.

Kafka depicted it in *The Penal Colony:* the punishment is to be strapped into the machine that cuts into living flesh, engraving on the prisoner himself, and thereby making known for the first time, both the sentence and the law itself.

Such a machine, contrived in the bush, is circumcision and clitoridectomy. Their supremely public character is essential to them, and contrasts with the scarification, cicatrization and tattooing one warrior, one woman, does on another. They appear, we already noted, as the high-point of tribal self-celebration, and efforts to abolish them, by missionaries, shepherds of foreign herds, or by public health officials, are resisted vehemently, as though the very existence of the tribal bond were at stake. Circumcision and clitoridectomy, done at twelve to fourteen years, and without anaesthesia or hygiene, is a torture done by the public in one's most sensitive and pleasure-producing zone. This incision pronounces and inscribes the sentence by which the public disposes of the individual. It is at the same time the means by which law, the prohibition and the oppression that is the essence of the gregarious order, is made known and comes to exist.

It is an operation that makes libidinal impulses into desire and want, through castration. For the circumcision castrates the male of the labia about his penis, as the clitoridectomy castrates the female of her penis. It is through castration of the natural bisexual that the social animal is produced. The marks now become signs, by which the intensive zones of one refer to, need, another. A memory, a mind, is being produced for the fugitive and capricious unconscious of the libidinal animal; and nothing was more cruel, more painful, Nietzsche wrote, than the mnemotechnics by which the savage animal gave itself a mind, a memory in which singular excitations are transformed into intrinsically generic signs.

* * *

How irritated Leni Riefenstahl was to find, after all that money and all that trouble to get there, with her ton and a half of gear, to show her Nuba the book she had made of them, that they were now wearing clothes! And Mirella Ricciardi, after publishing her international prize-winning photographic celebration of the Maasai initiation rites, to learn that the socialist government of Tanzania has now ordered them to wear pants! The texts each woman has written for her book tell the epic trouble they went through, transporting forty to fifty crates of equipment and supplies first by air cargo from Europe, then in Land-rovers and trucks which broke down and for which spare parts had to be procured from remote captials, the resources of ministries, generals, military outposts that had to be marshaled. To get to the "last of the Nuba," to "vanishing Africa." "That's it," Mirella Ricciardi writes, to conclude. "I don't ever want to go on safari again, at least for the moment. I dream of staying at home and looking after my children and growing flowers in my garden—I have to end my book some day—the time has come—I'm knocked out, shot, there's plenty of material for my book. I have nothing more to say. The car is up for sale. Kumuyu and Shaibu, go home and rest, thanks for standing by me as you did." But the dust jacket of her book informs us that Leni Riefenstahl is already back at it, shooting a documentary about her Nuba. With her five Leicas and motordrives and the 21, 28, 35, 50, 60 Macro, 90, 135, 180, 250, 400 and 560 mm lenses.

Why not stay in Germany, where almost anyone will take off his pants for whoever cares to look? Why not just take that comfortable and inexpensive train to Sylt, where healthy athletic Aryans run, washed clean by the North Sea? There was a time when Leni Riefenstahl was sufficiently electrified with Olympian nudity to half persuade the world to share her Nazi sex fantasies. Is it now only perversity that turns her on?

Oh, but it's not the same thing! One day in Rumsiki in the Camaroons Moravia jotted down in his diary: "All of a sudden an entire family, completely naked, issued from a little cavern half hidden by the trees. And not merely naked, but also disheveled, with hair standing on end, suggesting, as it were, the idea of the demented nudity that can sometimes be seen in lunatic asylums. The whole family, laughing frenziedly, threw themselves upon the car, offering for sale some little pipes made of chalk, of their own manufacture

41

and decidedly phallic in form. I noticed that their nakedness was made visible, so to speak, by their ugliness: they all had swollen paunches, their legs were thin and wrinkled and stiff; the woman's breasts were flabby and drooping—all of them things that were only noticeable one might say, because they were ugly. And so, as I looked at them, I realized that beauty is a kind of clothing, in other words, that a beautiful body is never truly naked. It is probable that nervous disorder, which in the so-called primitive peoples is just as severe (or even more so) as in the so-called civilized, expresses itself in ugliness; whereas beauty goes to indicate an absence of neuroticism."[5]

The German nudity is beautiful. With a beauty that is not just skin-deep. This nakedness does not expose a skin claiming to be attractive by the scars, welts, incisions, graphics or graffiti covering it. The German nakedness celebrates naturalness, what a German is by virtue of being born healthy and Aryan and vigorous, the beauty that is not decorative, rococo, but functional. The Bauhaus body, with broad ribs and biceps heroic, and proportion too, for that means poise, agility, freedom in movement. The body built: power, and delineation, that is, all the articulations of that power clear and distinct, and proportion. Breasts full and firm, thighs pivoting and loose, for moving on her own, and for strip-tease dancing. A male on his own, a female on her own. This nudity, and this beauty, and this naturalness exposes a body integral and functional, where the exposed exterior is one with the inner axes and drive shafts.

And it is hard. What is comparable to that feeling firm and full under one's skin? Mishima contrasted vehemently the vague, visceral, dark inwardness of the intellectual, loose and amorphous under his skin, with that feeling.[6] That phallic feeling. That Arnold Schwartzenegger feeling—of having a hard-on, the calves, the arms, the chest, the neck, being a hard-on, coming... That's the male denuding, on the beaches of Sylt, under the northern sun. The female is complementary.

It is not an erotogenic surface, spreading perversely its excitations over a closed body without organs beneath. It is body and soul one, nature and culture one, it is surface and depth one. It is the organism. A functional whole, coded from the inside.

And it is male, female. Human. Phallic. That is, the whole body organized, for the other. Which other? Alterity itself, the transcendent, the beyond? Shiva, Sita, Ngai, Agazu? Oh no, here we are *en famille*. For a mummy, for a big daddy. For Jocasta, for Agamemnon. For mummy, for daddy.

That is civilized nudity. It is also capitalist nudity. *Der Spiegel* features it every week; it goes with the Leicas and the Porsches.

There is, on the one hand, a going beyond the primary process libido to the organization man. The dissolute, disintegrated savage condition, with the perverse and monstrous extension of an erotogenic surface, pursuing its surface effects, over a closed and inert, sterile body without organs, one with the earth itself—this condition is overcome, by the emergence of, the dominion of, the natural and the functional. The sane body, the working body, free, sovereign, poised, whose proportion, equilibrium and ease are such that it dominates the landscape and commands itself at each moment. Mercury, Juno. Olympic ideal.

And, on the other hand, there has occurred a phallicization. Such a nakedness, healthy and sovereign, is at the same time nothing but the very image, the very presence of a lack. It calls for the other, for kisses and caresses, for the one that exists veritably qua lack-of-a-phallus. It cannot disrobe itself without being that visible, palpable lack, that want. We civilized ones feel not only a repugnance for the unnaturalness, the unhealthiness, the ugliness of that tattooed nakedness the savage affects; we find it puerile and shallow. The savage fixing his identity on his skin. Our identity is inward, it is our functional integrity as machines to produce a certain civilized, that is, coded, type of actions.

What then is this thing about savages? Who, instead of taking that train to the beaches of Sylt, flies off to the savages—with a ton and a half of gear, shipped air freight? Very civilized people, no? Capitalists.

To be sure capitalism goes everywhere, and goes to the savages too, to capitalize on them. The hour is late, in history; savagery cannot go on for much longer. It is the lot of savages to get civilized. To get despotized, first, tyrannized. Then colonized. Priests go to them, and colonels, on a mission, and executive managers, on safari. In short, capitalists, to civilize them.

But there are also some few nuts—schizophrenics—themselves highly civilized and capitalized, who go to them, in order to go back to or forward to savagery! Whose libido is such that that is what turns them on.

But they are the nuts of capitalism. Extra parts, surplus products produced by capitalist means of production.

In capitalism all the excitations, all the pleasures and the pains produced on the surface of life are inscribed, recorded, fixed, coded on the transcendent body of capital. Every pain costs something, every girl at the bar, every day off, every hangover, every pregnancy; and every pleasure is worth something. A man, as a sensuous being, is a commodity, Kant explained in *The Metaphysical Principles of Virtue,* whose "skill and diligence in labor have a market value; wit, lively imagination, and humor have a fancy value." "Even the fact that he excels [the other animals] in having understanding and can set up ends for himself still gives him only an external value for his usefulness, namely, the value of a man in preference to another animal. This is to say that he has a price as a commodity in the exchange of these animals as things, in which he still has a lower value than the general medium of exchange, money, whose value is therefore called preeminent *(pretium eminens)."*[7] The abstract and universal body of capital forms an improductive plenum upon which the excitations are bound, coded, circulated. They are no longer, as in the bush, inscribed on the bare surface of the earth. Nor on the body politic. At this advanced stage of capitalism one has lost a lot of regional, territorial, civic, professional identities; one becomes a succession of surface moments of subjectivity, pleasures and pains, forming and disintegrating at the surface where there are intensive couplings with what the flux of capital washes by.

The human, phallic protest is in reality a last-ditch expedient. This effort to congeal into a unit, a functional whole, and maintain that by one's own efforts, in the universal gym and on the bicycle that you ride without going anywhere, in your bathroom. And by this form of identity to be something someone needs. Not capitalism, of course, which just needs hands, and brains. Someone, a human being. A woman, lack of a phallus. A man, materialized phallus.

It is hard, though, to believe in all that. Where, after all, on the planet are still more human beings needed? All that is just a game, isn't it, on the already overcrowded beaches of Sylt? Capitalism looks on it with a kindly eye; coupled up with the Mercedes and the Mausers, it helps sell.

But away from the beaches, what gets produced is—at the limit—someone without real human or phallic identity, not male, not woman, not human, someone without central or functional identity, a certain extension of erotogenic surface, couplings with superfluous and surface things, with Suzukis, with Nikonos cameras, with Scuba tanks, with parasailing parachutes, with which there is produced the pleasure of driving, of consuming the miles, of covering the earth, of floating adrift in the sea, of being dragged through the sky. These couplings with the elemental do not feed into, do not serve the functional inner machinery of the working body. They are surplus potential, accumulating on the surface, consumed by local and momentary egoisms. What is beneath, what is the full and sated body upon whose surface they effervesce? An anonymous, sterile and inert body, a certain stock whose worth is determined by the universal body without organs of capital which measures everything and distributes all the pleasures and pains. Itself just a fund of capital, then. This kind of dehumanized, dephallicized, insignificant entity is the final product of capitalism. I was going to say: this kind of subjectivity—but what there is here is not a subjectivity, but a split, fragmented, dismembered, disintegrated field of momentary subjectivities, forming in pleasure and pain. Schizophrenicized subjectitity.

And it is this kind of schizo personality that goes off to the savages. Not to live with them as among brothers and sisters. Not to find real men, and real women, finally, to fill up that aching hole, that phallic lack one has made of oneself. But to feel the sun in the empty savanna, to stand in antedeluvian landscapes unmarked by all history, malignant bush country, whitish plains without contour or dimensions where there is nothing moving but the termites and the tsetse flies, the squalor of eternity.

And to collect pictures, some beads and neck hangings, some fetishes, some warthog's teeth, to stick in one's mouth, to suck, and to get in some hours flying a private twoseater over the Mountains of the Moon, parasailing alongside the Indian Ocean, scuba-diving in equatorial waters. Putting together one's own pleasure chains, out of the debris of civilization, not according to its codes, by bricolage. Like savages do.

But driven by a libido that wants to wander off to the land where there are those who are kissed by the green mamba, who are strong enough to be chosen by, and to hold the embrace of, the leopard.

Notes

1. Leni Riefenstahl, *The People of Kau* (London: Collins, 1976), p. 7.
2. Mirella Ricciardi, *Vanishing Africa* (London: Collins, 1974).
3. Gilles Deleuze & Félix Guattari, *Anti-Oedipus*, trans. by Robert Hurley, Mark Seem, and Helen R. Lane (New York: Viking, 1977), pp. 9-15.
4. *Op. cit.*, p. 145.
5. Alberto Moravia, *Which Tribe Do You Belong To?* (New York: Farrar, Straus and Giroux, 1974), p. 212-213.
6. Yukio Mishima, *Sun and Steel*, trans. John Bester (New York: Grove, 1970), p. 23.
7. Immanuel Kant, *The Metaphysical Principles of Virtue*, trans. by James Ellington (Indianapolis & New York: Bobbs-Merrill, 1964), pp. 96-97.

Khajuraho

ANOTHER WAY A HINDU'S PRAYER DIFFERS FROM A EUROPEAN'S IS this—and it is an essential difference: a Hindu prays naked, as naked as possible, only covering his chest or stomach if he is of weak health.

Decency is not at stake. He prays alone in darkness beneath the immobile world.

There should be no intermediary, no clothing between oneself and the Whole; one should in no way feel divided from one's body.

A Hindu also likes to pray in water, while bathing.

A Hindu who in my presence was making his prayer to Kali took off all clothing but a small waistband and said to me, "When I pray alone at sunset, and naked, I pray more easily."

All clothing separates one from the world. Whereas stretched out, naked in the darkness, the Whole flows over you, and draws you into its breath.

Making love with his wife, a Hindu thinks of God of which she is an expression and a part.

How beautiful it must be to have a woman who understands that, who spreads immensity over the small but so troubling and decisive spasm of love, over this sudden and great abandon.

This communion in the immense, at such a moment of common pleasure, must be truly an experience that enables one to look at people in the eyes, with a magnetism that cannot withdraw, holy and lustral at once, impudent and shameless; even an animal must communicate with God, they say, so much is limitation, whatever it be, odious to them.

Excesses

There are even Hindus who masturbate while thinking of God. They say it would be worse to make love with a woman (in the European way) who individualizes you too much and does not know how to pass from the idea of love to that of Everything.

Henri Michaux

Here is yet another way the erotic impulse is equivocal: on the one hand, it is exclusionary; two lovers are shut up in their passion, ensnared in one another, closed to the world and deaf to its causes. The carnal passion draws all the faculties of life into an obsessive and jealous absorption in one singular individual, and even one singular trait or turn of that individual. But there is also a tendency of sensuality to spread, to generalize. It turns the most unlikely things into analogies or figures of lust, so as to be able to excite itself anywhere; it even, in the case of fetishes, can displace itself entirely onto things remote from any possibility of sexual interaction. It is as though the libidinous impulse is an exorbitant energy that tends not to satisfy itself and subside, like other desires and appetites, but to excite itself with its own want, feeding on its hunger. It seems lust can hardly be held to its own direction or its own function; everything gets infected with its trouble, even practical associations to work with tools, political relationships within institutions, pedagogical relationships over ideas, military alliances before the imminence of disaster and in the thirst for conquest. Not only can the pursuit of riches or the investiture with political authority function as a means to obtain partners of flesh and blood, but cupidity and calculation themselves become lascivious. One can see uniforms, napalm, mutilated bodies with the lusts that behold hardened penis, burning loins, sprawled out thighs. One can feel the contemplative bliss which pure thought and reasoning produce over and beyond any of the practical satisfactions they may lead to to have analogies no doubt based on nature with voluptuous abandon.

The sense of the equivocation in the sexual drive is at the core of the Platonic and Freudian theories of sublimation. That is, the hypothesis that the search for knowledge, the striving for justice, the

longing for beauty, the metaphysical nostalgia for unity and wholeness in the diversity and the transience of experience owe their force
to genital rather than cerebral drives, represent transformations of or
disguises of libido.

In the *Symposium* the Socratic inquiry after the definition and the
essence of love turns into a history of love. A youth begins by falling
in love with another youth, but this erotic attachment is as it were
not contented with itself; in the very measure that it is not frustrated,
is free to be, it goes beyond itself. It was an exclusive attachment to
an individual close to oneself, homophile, seeking yet more closeness.
But in the measure that it intensifies, it loses what was exclusive and
particular in it. It spreads horizontally, becoming an attachment to
boy after boy, to men, to women. And it reaches vertically, toward
the general, the universal, the pure forms.

Eros neither begins nor ends as a faculty to ensure the reproduction
of the species or as a craving for immediate sensual gratification. Far
from being a corporeal mechanism, it is activated by a telos, is
purposive; its forces come from the ultimate and most remote end,
that of the radiance of the unending. Indeed eros is the purposive in
general. It is erotic force in every human operation that animates it
with teleology, with a longing for the beyond. Then, paradoxically, ✓
it is philosophical dialectics that is the apt method to know the true
nature of sensual lust.

There is in us an impetuous will to reach the total order of things.
This urge does not originate in practical perplexities; it arises by a
spread, a generalization, of erotic impulses. Its most comprehensive
form, philosophy, is at bottom an erotic craving, a form of love of
the universe. The science of eros is philosophic self-understanding.

Freud, too, explained the most sublime by the most carnal.
Resisting the Socratic identification of truth with the good, of
curiosity with virtue, he sensed something devouring, penetrating, ✓
violating in the craving to know. There is in the man of knowledge
not simply a disinterested, contemplative will for the truth for the
sake of the truth; there is also a sort of peeping tomism, a
scoptophilia, a compulsion to uncover, to undress everything, a

compulsion to get on top of things, to violate them, to divulge their secrets, to penetrate into them. The mind of the explorer is made of the infantile voracity that attacks the maternal body, extension of the breast, to steal the contents of that body, especially the siblings it contains, to jealously destroy them and to amorously penetrate and fill the maternal womb. This infantile aggressivity which gives rise to the guilty fear of putting the mother to death itself leads the infant to detach itself from the mother and displace its energies onto other spheres of exploitation.

Similarly Freud found libidinal compulsions under the striving for justice. The modern secularized state responsible for the general welfare, first of all economic, of its citizens, is an outgrowth of associations for armed force and for establishing values in a human grouping, an outgrowth of military and mythico-ritual, or ecclesiastical, associations. What motivates military enterprises may be considerations of survival, or predatory instincts, but what creates lasting military associations characterized by loyalty and internal submission, and not only bands that, as among animals, find safety or force in numbers, is strong homoerotic feeling. A church is not merely an association of men holding common convictions; what is specific to this sort of organization is that the members love one another. And the members are not only students of the founder or leader, but love him as children love a father.

Freud sought an erotic basis to the attachment to beauty, too. As our dreams by night visualize a symbolic gratification of our desires, especially our erotic appetites, so the production of artworks is a deliberate and waking dreamwork, an idealizing elaboration of phantasms, hallucinatory gratification of erotic longings. Art is made of the artifices of love.

For Plato the free eros tends, of itself, to sublimate, to leave the intimate to ascend to the universal and the eternal. Its extension, its horizontal spread, is not only accompanied by, but made possible by, its comprehension, its vertical ascent. This teleology, this striving ever onward and upward, belongs to its nature. The erotic factor is the transcending movement, is the desire in all desires, its own nature is the movement toward universal nature; through our erotic craving we open our lives progressively to a love of all things. The philosophic life, the contemplative fascination with the universal order of all things and in all things, blissful state of wisdom without any utilitarian or subjugating will, is the final form of eroticism, is universal love.

Freud's positivist concept of libido is divested of all teleology. Libido is not a lack, a *penia*, that ceaselessly seeks the unending, but an excess tension that tends to neutralize itself and is unending because it has no ends; it is desire without being desire for something, desire for nothing or desire to be nothing, compulsion of an excess to discharge itself. The sex urge is not naturally a craving of a male for a female; it is culture, repression, and taboos, that will narrow it down to a certain sex object. Originally the sex urge in an infant is capable of attaching itself onto anything—another human of the same or of different sex, an animal, an object, oneself, a part of another being or of oneself. There is no natural direction in the intrinsic restlessness of the libidinous tension. And there is not that upward striving, that natural movement from more base to more and more sublime objects of love as in Plato, a movement toward the more comprehensive forms that would make possible its empirical extension. For Freud the extension of the libidinal impulse is due to its lack of a telos. He speaks not only of an original polymorphousness, but also of an original perversity. The libidinal impulse is dismembering rather than integrating, wanton and not purposive, profaning and violating and not issuing in contemplative bliss.

Then for Freud sublimation is the result of repression. It is because the originally wild, unbound sexual attachment of the infant is repressed that it seeks outlets in the sublime forms of a search for knowledge, a striving after just, that it, fraternal and loving, society, and a longing for beauty, that is, universal or culturally acceptable phantasms. The ultimate metaphysical oneness and wholeness the erotically driven life seeks is the unavowable intimacy of the infantile condition, prior to all culture.

Indeed it is the absence of the oral plenitude or the anal loss, and later the phallic want, that are the cores about which reality, objects autonomous and objectives, are originally constituted. It is not the enduring forms, but the lack in forms, that objectifies the flux of appearances. The motor of objectification, and finally what drives a human to seek restlessly to understand the whole universe, is the frustration of immediate gratification.

The original forms of social organization, military and religious, cover libidinal interests; one seeks love in them, they are not simply practical or intellectual-axiological cooperatives. But the sensuality involved is repressed. It is the force of libidinal bonding, stronger than the pain of the servile depersonalization and mechanization, that molds lusty virility into soldiery uniformity. That homoeroticism must always be there, and always be repressed; the Platonic army of real lovers has never existed. So also for the church: the proof that you are a Christian is not that you are intellectually persuaded of a certain list of doctrines; it is, the Evangelist says, "See how they love one another!" The oceanic religious feeling is this erotic bond, intense but diffuse, but which must be unavowed and unactualized; the specifically ecclesiastical morality is a systematic negation of the law of the flesh.

Similarly in art: the spell of its perfect colors and forms, its elusive and unconceptualizable movements, insinuates while dissembling the night of concupiscence. The artistic genius is this ingenuity. The Mona Lisa must not leer at you—just that enigmatic, ineffable smile, equivocal and suggestive, where avid sensuality trembles in devoted and reserved tenderness. Art is not elicited teleologically by the radiance of the eternal forms, but engendered by the deviousness of the carnal. Beauty for Freud is not the telos of eros, but its travesty. "The genitals, the sight of which provokes the greatest sexual excitement, can never really be considered 'beautiful.' "[1]

A theory of sublimation takes sexuality out of the biological order to find sensuality everywhere as the motor force of intellectual, ethical, aesthetic and metaphysical culture. Eroticism is not a biological drive which has as its natural and normative finality the propagation of the given species. The fascination with and temptation to bestiality, the transgression of one's own natural species, appears as old as culture itself; it is modern culture that is humanist, the ancient cultures were pursuits in the direction of the ultra-human, totemic metamorphoses or divinization. Within the given species, the horror of confusion between the two natural biological relations—male and female complementarity, parent and offspring dependency—expressed in the horror of incest is undermined by the adult-adult dependency and same sex complementarity upon which physical or moral authority institutions are built. These institutions demand, in every case of conflict, sacrifice of natural family bonds. There is even in Greek tragic theater a kind of sacred fascination with incest in the wake of this entry into institutional history.

Theories of sublimation, which see the libido as a polymorphous urge that has in itself a compulsion to seek ever new forms of realization or of release, undermine the idea of a biological norm in sexuality, but they also undermine every idea of a norm throughout culture. Neither nature nor culture has its norm in its proper forms. For Freud not only does desire have no natural object or natural enactment, but our libidinal nature is inevitably—naturally— frustrated in the direction it takes. If he admits a progression toward heterosexual maturity, where biological propagation of the species is in fact ensured, this heterosexuality is built on a homosexual identification with the father, this maturity made of the accumulation of infantile overestimations and overdeterminations, this reproductive copulation made of anal, oral and Oedipal gratifications. Of its own nature the libido is ceaselessly frustrated, and ceaselessly inventive; it lives and vitalizes only in anaclitic investments and circumlocutions. Cultural products then can never have their norms and ends in their own natures; they are essentially detours, deviations, dissimulations.

For Plato precisely what is natural is that the erotic craving is teleological, that something in it never be satisfied with the particular and with immediate gratification, that it always contain the urge to go further. What it seeks from the beginning Plato will name with words "beauty" and "immortality"—immortal beauty and beautiful immortality. For there is a beauty that looks immortal, that is the very vision of immortality—beauty made of proportion, harmony, equilibrium, form which of itself has no longer any inner lacks or irresolution, classical beauty. And eternity is of itself splendid, effulgent, cosmos that makes the chaos chaotic, order that makes of the disordered this realm of the ceaselessly generating and corrupting. The tendency to exceed every structure or term, until it attains the unending, this drive that of itself pushes on until it would be transported by the pure effulgence of the rapturous, is eros's very nature. When eros reaches this final normative order, it has left behind all its sensuality and become metaphysical.

Man's soul, said Aristotle, is by its nature destined to open upon, and to somehow be, all things. It is the universe as such that is the proper object of the congenital craving in man's nature. The theories of sublimation seat this universal destination in the drive that, in naturalist and in biological thinking, would be the factor by which the human species conserves just itself.

The theories of sublimation are thus theories of universal love. But they also formulate a universal self-negation of love.

For Freud if the polymorphously perverse libido has no natural object, it itself has a nature, a proper realization: it is a tropism of release, of immediate gratification. The Freudian analysis is not a phenomenology but a physics: the libido is not equal to the succession of its forms; it is the invariant force behind all of them, a force ever transforming forms but never itself transformed. Because it is always the same eros behind all the cultural forms, however elaborated, however far extended, all the cultural goals can never be anything but detours, ever more immensely remote deferrings of the natural goal. Thus sublimation is not only the result of repression; it is itself repression. High culture does not represent the ever more rich satisfaction of man's protean desiring nature but the ever more extensive dissimulation of its demand. As eros becomes ever more universal, and, in civilization, ever more conscious and capable, it turns ever more into a discontent.

Plato's account, despite all its mythical etiologies, is essentially a phenomenology. Plato lines up the forms of love in an ever expanding succession, and eros itself is nothing but the pure transformation of these forms. The self-transcending of eros is both horizontal and vertical; this exclusive attachment to the particular of its own intensity, of its own energy, moves from particular to particular and also from particular to universal, from phenomenal forms to essential form, from transitory to eternal. This movement is already in the first erotic attachment: from the first eros seeks the form in the appearance, eternity in the ephemeral, the absolute in the relative and relational. It sense is from the first metaphorical. The vertical ascent of eros is valued over the horizontal extension. It is the sublimation of desire and not promiscuity that Platonism values. Value indeed is the very establishment of verticality. Finally it is philosophy that is the highest and ultimate form of love and the life most to be loved. For it is love of the most general, the most universal: the pure order, of itself eternal, in the universe. Here philosophy is the fulfillment of desire, and high culture the fulfillment of nature.

For Plato the gaze that first fixes on a youth and becomes erotic— and it is especially the gaze that is erotic—is not *attendrissement*, moved, afflicted by the vulnerability, the mortality of youth, but fixed, stabilized by the harmony and proportion of youth, as yet unmarked by life's battles and defeats. It is not love for the generating and corrupting, for youth and transience, but love for the eternal. Plato sees in the first sensuous rapture fascination with beauty, that is, with eternity, with the immobilization of a form in its own perfection. What is sensual in the organic function is an aesthetic sensibility.

It is this same aesthetic essence, found again in the cognitive life, that makes possible the continuity Plato will trace in them, and makes possible his erotic conception of intellectual life. For him knowing is not a practical problem-solving operation, it is not an exercise of power; its highest and perfect form is contemplative. It has its own bliss, which is that of contemplating the order, the logos, the all-encompassing and abiding forms of the universe. Apollonian bliss.

The Platonic theory of sublimation brings into view a conceptual mode of eros. It is the grasping of the universal in the particular, the form in the appearance, the closure of the ideal in the transience of the generating and corrupting, that makes eros a transcendence, a becoming, a drive. Understanding as intuition—immediate appropriation of a perfect and closed form—requires and makes possible discursivity. But discursivity requires the closure of forms, the positing of the universal beyond the particular, in order to move. There is an understanding in eros from the first, a conceptual understanding, and it is this comprehension that destines eros in man to its sublime cultural extension.

Nietzsche has shown that this understanding was contrived by Platonism to supplant the Dionysian, tragic, understanding. Dionysian understanding is a sensibility for the moving forces beneath, or in, the forms, and for the fortuity and gratuity of those forces. The Dionysian practice of understanding is not contemplative and comprehending, but discerning, disconcerted and differentiating. For Plato metaphysical understanding goes beyond such tragic sensibility, and it is precisely eros that propels it beyond.

But when it goes beyond, does it comprehend any longer the specific nature of the sensual drive? It leads beyond a youth and beyond youth, beyond love of the generating and corrupting, love of youth, transitory love of transience; it goads to a contemplative bliss beyond the mortal saturation of every orgasm. Philosophy shows that the sensual craving in fact craves the final chaste contemplative bliss of a metaphysical life. This metaphysical love is but an erotic metaphor.

Could one then imagine an eroticism that would spread everywhere, invade all the domains of high culture, and not be a contagion of misery, not be driven by frustration? An eroticism that would sensualize the mind in its quest for the truth of the real, that would infect the political order, that would intensify through artifices and in art, and that would be nowhere dissimulated or dissimulating, but discover its climactic intensity in the most sublime forms?

To visualize such a thing, it is enough to go visit Khajuraho, in central India, and its wonderful temples. Of the eighty-five temples built there in the tenth and eleventh centuries, twenty-two remain, but, put together without mortar out of precision cut granite or fine-grained sandstone blocks and covered with highly polished carvings, when the jungle was cleared from them a century and a half ago, they reemerged in astonishingly intact condition. They themselves tell us almost all we can know about the Chandella kingdoms which reigned for four centuries in this region a thousand years ago, and traced their descent from Chandra, the moon. Their blissful silence in this today almost completely uninhabited zone tells a singular tale of eros.

The temples are intricate assemblages of porticos, cones, drums, towers, stalagmites, across which the mind is invited to follow the derivations of and correlations between a vast number of abstract forms which a sovereign logico-mathematical intelligence has elaborated here. But this abstract geometry embraces within itself layer upon layer of friezes where what seems to be a universal combinatorium of carnal positions is brought to the same explicitness and precision. Auto-erotic stimulation, dual and multiple cunnilinctio, penilinctio, copulation, homosexual and bestial intercourse circulate about the temple walls, without primacy of place or of artistry given to any figure. There is nowhere suggestion of audacity or provocation, the leers that would suggest civic taboos being violated in the sacred precincts. Within the erotic there is not selection of with whom and for what being taught, but an extensive intelligence deriving all the possibilities and an artist sensibility perfecting the form and equilibrium of each mode. The temples tell us of a society that existed among men where sexual repression was once, but completely, unknown.

Although it is true that the temple, depiction of the cosmic Mount Meru, is conceived as a microcosm, it is not true that this is a logic that required an exposition of all animal and spirit intercourse, and requires their exteriority. When the worshipper penetrates the inner sanctuary of the temple, it has nothing to show him but the lingam—

and a few more erotic carvings. While contemplation of the lingam, utterly stylized phallic emblem, is, bringing the mind to the most integrated and unrepresenting state, the supreme metaphysical exercise, in fact it is not really different from the contemplative stasis at which the copulations outside are maintained. The sensual is nowhere transcended; even the highest intelligence and the last metaphysical rapture are voluptuous. Apsarases disrobing, yawning, rincing their hair, removing a thorn from a foot, playing with pets, writing letters, applying cosmetics are carved on the same height, with the same prominence and artistic exaltation as supreme gods Vishnu the preserver and Shiva the destroyer.

These then are veritable temples of love—but in what sense? They are not incitements to sex—civic-magical inculcations of fertility or palaces where phallocratic power is glorified. For the statuary depicts neither procreation nor even orgasm; on the contrary it is a blissful state of erotic charge maintained in a lucid and tenacious fever and vibrantly displayed that we especially see. The artistic exaggeration of genitalia proper to pregnancy and fertility cults does not occur here, and many of the tableaux depict non-impregnating manipulations. And the dissymmetry of the sexes does not become a practice of power and dependency. Penile erection is not generalized into male ascendancy, as in the art that casts secondary gender characteristics—male chest and male musculature—into the image of tumescence, nor does it become the concrete symbol, the very concretion of verticality and value.[2] Khajuraho shows men receiving female initiative, lying upside down beneath women, and the male figure, supple and pliant, coils and breathes rather than hardens into muscular erection, or into pillars about which the female would twine, seeking phallic support.

Where, we wonder, in the unrepressedly sensual soul here celebrated did this civilization derive its civilizing rigor? A thousand years of monsoon and jungle have not been able to take apart the mortarless cohesion of these precision cut edifices. The society that built them could only have been one in which craft and technical skills were valued and developed to a superior degree. There is nothing vegetative or baroque in their design, and they are not just tableaux vivants of erotic encounters; the representations form friezes on constructions where a staggeringly complicated, but everywhere mastered geometry commands. This is not an architecture that has resulted from a monumentalizing of utilitarian and profane construction, and the temples are not Mount Meru by virtue of any natural analogy of form. The new cosmic formula concretized in each was rather produced by an automous constructive intelligence.

The unity of purpose of the site, the highest standards of craft maintained in all details, and the prodigality of the effort—there were eighty-five temples, many with over five hundred statues—tell us that the Chandella moon kings who ruled here maintained an exceptionally powerful and exceptionally noble political order. But these are not monuments to secular power, and these are not carvings of divinized rulers; they are works of religion, of Jainism and Brahmanism, the religions theoretically and metaphysically most elaborated. To look at the temples is to convince oneself that the society that built them was one of exceptional pragmatic and technical achievement, of intense social purpose not maintained through divinization of secular power, of widely diffused abstract and gratuitous intelligence.

But here craft, engineering, architecture, social organization, mathematical intelligence, religious mysticism were not advances beyond, nor detours from, but new heights and realms for eroticism. These are not temples of love in that the culture knew nothing higher to enshrine than biological functions; they are temples in which sensuality itself reaches a supreme degree of intelligence, thoughtfulness, beauty, capable of entering into or assembling the cosmos.

Indeed rarely has man assumed a more ennobled visage than in this rock. These men and women closed in passionate embraces have brows poised with respect and gazes emanating intelligence, mouths trembling with susceptibility and lips benevolent and responsive, fingers ungrasping and reverent. Here there is nothing guilty or crafty, nothing disfigured with leering and duplicity, nothing self-indulgent or self-ashamed. There is nothing servile. They are blissful with the freedom of gods who have understood everything.

These bodies are not just writhing about like a tangle of worms. Each tableau is not an orgy but an asana. Is not nobility a physiological, vital, rather than civic virtue? In these hundreds of figures we see all that humans have found to be noble in the wingspread of eagles, in the langour of a tiger, in the coiling of a scorpion, in the watery freedom of fish, in the intensity of a cobra ready to strike.

And the human body here does not only, in its orgasmic intensity, contract every organic form, it does so to the point of carnal intercourse with every form of body. The temple frieze is the place where a carnal visage of all things is divined, is caressed. In animals: there is not in yoga which seeks to know and to stand, soar or creep with animal perfection the sense that one debases oneself to make love with scorpions, swans, bitches and boars. In things: the sanctuary finds a carnal visage to vines, to trees, to flowers, to mountains and fields; men release their seminal fluids in the holy Ganga, cosmic river which, in what we have named the Milky Way, is seen to flow across the night, to descend upon the celestial Himalayas in what we see as their snows, to pour across the plains where humankind's most ancient continuous civilization was elaborated, to carry the ashes of its generations to the oceans, to descend too into a subterranean Ganga coursing across the underworld before it reemerges again in the most remote heavens. Men pour their semen into this white sideral river; women open their wombs to the moon, to the sun, to the lonely and perfect stars. The carnal yearning embraces not only all terrestrial, but also the heavenly bodies. At Konarak it is thousands of lovers that form the chariot of Surya, the sun, whose movement across the heavens engenders all that is carnal, but is itself composed of the thousand movements of carnal desire. Here one neither descends, when one makes love with animals and trees, nor ascends, when one makes love with the moon, the rivers, the stars; one travels aimlessly or circularly about a universe eroticized.

The temples maintain the instability of the erotic gaze, shifted by its own intensity from form to form. We can see into the nature of this volatility when we consider what the carving in stone here has done to the orgasmic body, holding it in an aesthetic display. At first, when we shift our gaze into an aesthetic and no longer simply lusty appreciation of this spectacle, we try to catch on to the inner axes of these male and female bodies. For while we do know of an aesthetics of the color, the texture, the density of flesh, in sculpture that looks as classical as this we rather feel invited to catch on to a line of poise in the posture. It is for us not pure symmetry and relationship of shapes that constitutes the beauty of the human body, but the sense of life that we intuit in it, the invisible dynamic axis that the visible forms fixed statically intimate. And it is the agility, freedom, grace or sovereignty of a manner of dealing with or moving across the world intimated by that dynamic axis that captivates and communicated within us its delight.

But such is not the aesthetics of Khajuraho. The eyes of an Apsaras are fish.

The human form is here not treated as a single design whose spatial configuration expresses statically a dynamical axis or nexus of force. The sublimating erotic treatment is first of all a dismembering: her eyebrows are taut bows, her buttocks swelling gourds, her lips a sesamum petal. Faces are lotuses; jewel strings are water birds. The impassioned gaze is held successively upon each of the disjointed parts of the body, each perfect in itself, with the perfection of something extrahuman. And the eyes depicted are liquid, due to the way the carvers allow the eye surface to follow the length of the lids, rather than hold an independent sphericality. Fingers are comets descending from the sky, the gauzy clothes ripple off in streams. Unlike in Plato, the erotic gaze does not move from the human figure to the universal forms, but to sequences of particular forms which, having no common form, are metonymic and not metaphorical. A Gandharva's chest is the face of a cow, his arms are plantain-tree trunks, his kneecap the back of a crab.

That is why the men of Khajuraho do not personalize, for example, "power" and the women "grace." We do not see on the walls of Khajuraho something like a *virtus*-virility-activity and femininity-receptivity complementarity. It is true that the women of

Khajuraho are clinging, yielding and twining; but it is not true that the men are therefore trees about which these vines are seeking support. We see Shiva upside-down beneath women, supported by women, or all entangled.

What Hindu physiology in general prizes is suppleness, the ability to twist, to arch, to double-joint, to contract innumerable extra-human postures. The 8,400,000 asanas of Patanjali's classical hatha-yoga codify the 8,400,000 forms of animal positions there are—all taken as human possibilities. Khajuraho's yoga studies the torsion of the spine as Apsarases turn to look backward, to kiss and perform fellatio, to look down at the upturned sole of a foot. High on the shikkara of each temple is the heraldic image of the Chandellas—androgene holding the crouching power of a colossal leogryph, human heart held against beast's heart, the human body coiling with the same curvature as the leonine spine.[3] On the temple friezes this confrontation is repeatedly depicted with the vyalas—leonine figures with the heads of tigers, elephants, horses, bears, bulls, deer, parrots—that alternate everywhere with the figures of gods, lovers and Apsarases.

What is being celebrated here is the serpent power, kundalini. The yoga serpent is not the phallic figure of the comparative anthropologists. As it rises in the passionate body, it also coils into the six chakras, lotuses, rather than thrust from the glans penis. Love's art traces another itinerary here from in the West—not from head down—and stops to illuminate each chakra as it rises. The beauty that smoulders in these coils is not that of the one and the essence, the metaphysical or metaphorical eternal constant.

Toes, thighs, arms, tongues pressing, the figures of Khajuraho hold one another in erotic ardor, and gaze passionately into one another's eyes. The look gazes into eyes, without seeking a term or a telos, without seeking fertility or orgasmic release, without seeking. Their gaze is without posturing, conventions or defenses, liquid and free, fish, braced up by nothing, holding on to nothing. Next to the couple stands an Apsaras, her opulent hips poised in their disequilibrated provocation, her nudity glittering with jewels, the ardor of kundalini coiling and circling, determining each detail of her composition. She is looking, with the same gaze, into a mirror.

What do these transfixed eyes see? Does this kundalini serpent gaze look upon the eroticized body of the embraced to there get deflected down all the metonymic series, down all the perfect forms of nature, in ever widening sequences, see fish and sesamum buds and praying mantises and hungry eagles and exploding galaxies? Does not this serpentine embrace hold the briny composition of the sea in blood, with its strange glands and polyps? Do not these gauzy garments ripple over coral reefs and dark waters, behind the eyes of the beloved, flash of silver, play of fish?

This gaze then does not, like that of Socrates's Diotima, transcend the sensuous membrane to ascend to the one and the essence; it is shattered and scattered by the fish eyes of the Apsaras in all the directions where the perfect things materialize and turn. And finally it even returns to itself nonetheless.

For here the standing Apsaras, tense and languid, contemplates herself in a mirror with the same eyes, seeing what the adjacent couple sees in the mirror of one another's eyes—not oneself but series of the universe, not forms but flash of silver in the dark waters, or delight.

Here pleasure is not being conceived in the psychoanalytic way, as the immediacy of sense gratification, and tension release. On all the tableaux of Khajuraho the intensity of the serpent charge is being maintained. It is sustained because what is immediately disclosed in carnal contact is the most remote and strange things, scorpion, sea anemone, comet in oneself. As the Apsaras contemplates her own body, the kundalini rises, her body coils with its own ardor. "Here is the Ganges and the Jumna...here are Prayaga and Benares—here the sun and the moon. Here are the sacred places, here the Pithas and the Upa-pithas—I have not seen a place of pilgrimage and an abode of bliss like my body."[4] This gaze that finds Benares and the Ganges, the sun and the moon in her body, this gaze deflected across the rivers and down the astral orbits, is dispersed and scattered not by frustration of a primary sense pleasure, but by its very intensity. And the subterranean constellations and celestial rivers, the places of pilgrimage and the figures of reincarnation are not dissimulations of a carnal libido, but discoveries of the kundalini fire itself which renders them carnal; this then is why the awakening of the serpent power culminates in this poised gaze and no longer issues in orgasmic tension release.

If the carvings of Khajuraho engrave an entirely different destiny of the libido from what Freudianism teaches, this form of sublime carnality is also not that of Platonism. What the eroticized gaze contemplates is not the splendor of the intelligible order, appropriated by a comprehensive contemplation. Here the beauty of the partner is dismembered into an unending sequence of animal and vegetative and crystalline forms, each closed in its own perfection. It is at once the enchanted discovery that the singularity of each strange form of nature is perfect. The beauty of this face is the beauty of the sesamum bud, of the swelling gourds, of the fluttering water birds, of the floating polyps discovered in it, by the disconcerted gaze, by these fish eyes delighting in these dark waters. Where what delights is the flash of the ephemeral, the evanescent. These eyes do not see in the necklace that Apsaras bound by the chain of ageless stones; they see a flight of water birds.

This serpent does not long for the eternity Platonism longs for and catches sight of in the self-containment of the comprehensive forms. It is held in the stasis of the atelic erotic intensity. All yoga seeks this instant of stasis in the cycles of time, nirvanic instant. Diotima shows Socrates the eternity of forms fixed before the restless erotic gaze; Khajuraho shows the unending metamorphoses of forms before a gaze fixed in its own intensity.

But if the carnal contact is visionary, this contemplation is copulative—and to have intercourse with a man or a woman is already to have intercourse with crab and bird, gorgonian and star. The Platonic soul, contemplating the self-subsistence, the immortality of the beautiful forms, seeks to be fixed in its own form, immortalized in its own identity. There are Tantric bronzes in Nepal and Tibet where one would see, if one separated the embraced couple, the man now bearing vulva and the woman penis.

And what, then, is this artist will, that has carved this bliss forgotten centuries ago in the jungles of Madhya Pradesh as our civilization constructed its cenotaphs? Why carve this glandular and fluid sensuality in this rock? Why this petrification, if not out of a will to eternalize the fugitive spasm of carnal love?

But very likely the question also expresses our Platonic-metaphysical nostalgias. Is not the supreme feat of eroticism here—that which demanded these carvings, these temples—to render the stone itself passionate, rather than passion petrified? Hindu sculpture does not, like Hellenistic art, bring the petrified into life by carving out tensions and counter-tensions in musculature, in the mechanism of bones and sinews, as though life is force or will-power. Rather here the chest, torso and limbs are smooth and loose, like glands, accentuated by the sharp carving of ornament against the smoothness of skin—chains and necklaces, water birds taking flight. They breathe; it is *aspiration* that the sculpturing genius has engraved in the stone, that and not force and self-movement is the gravity of life that afflicts and weighs in the mineral substances out of which it is composed. And that is also why this carving is passionate, all the coils and smooth surfaces of the forms invite the touch of the sighing lips and the breath-light touch of the caress. But of course the carving is especially a vision. To be looked at, with eyes. With eyes of fish, of happiness.

Notes

1. Sigmund Freud, *Three Essays on the Theory of Sexuality*, trans. James Strachey (London: Hogarth, 1953), Vol. VII, p. 156n.
2. The relationship between phallocentric culture and the institution of the

dimension of verticality and value in metaphysical thought was first perceived by Jacques Lacan (*Ecrits* [Paris: Seuil, 1966], pp. 685-686) and Jacques Derrida (*La dissémination* [Paris: Seuil, 1972,], pp. 56-57).

3. See Frontispiece.
4. Shashi Bhusan Dasgupta, *Obscure Religious Cults as Background of Bengali Literature* (Calcutta: Univ. of Calcutta, 1946), pp. 103-104.

The Rangda

Children of the Sun

ON CHRISTMAS DAY OF 1872 NIETZSCHE WROTE TO COSIMA Wagner: "In some far corner of the universe lost in the scintillations of innumerable solar systems, there was one day a star upon which animals endowed with intelligence invented knowledge. It was the proudest and most deceptive moment of universal history, but it was only a moment. Nature had hardly had time to breathe when that star froze over, and the intelligent animals had to die. Indeed their time had come, for though they had flattered themselves that they had already accumulated vast knowledge, they came, to their great disappointment, to discover that at bottom all their knowledge was false. They perished and disappeared with the death of truth. Such was the lot of those animals doomed to despair, who had invented knowledge."[1]

Is there, then, emnity between the systems of reason and that of suns? Reason is reckoning, calculation of equivalences. Reason could operate with just anything whatever, with fictions and illusions, but it is serious when it operates with the force and substance of reality. A fund of force and substance lends itself to rational calculation when it constitutes a closed system wherein changes and exchanges are compensated for.

The intelligent social orders set up by rational animals on the surface of the dead star constitute closed economic systems. Their intelligent laws are contrived for the purpose of the regulation of wealth. The problem, in what rational animals call civilization, is the production, circulation and conservation of wealth.

The economics that reasoning animals elaborate for the closed systems of their civilization is a special economics, valid within these systems. These systems, however, are not self-contained. We can name general economics the study of the laws of wealth generally.

Upon us and our closed systems the sun hurls out of itself 3.8×10^{33} ergs/sec.; this immense conflagration is the source and the very substance of virtually all the reality and all the wealth circulating in this area of the universe. The force of this radiation drives all the movements and combinations in this zone; its movement is found in them. Were we to envisage laws of wealth from the universal point of view, we should discover that the first law of a generalized economy of solar wealth is expenditure without recompense.

The sun is as it were in excess relative to itself. The problem, at the source and essence of wealth, is one of expenditure. The sun destines all its forces to annihilation; it is burning itself out as fast as it can. It squanders its enormous energy, most of which is lost in the emptiness. The crystalline and mental systems, which have taken form about the sun and reflect its radiance, owe their origin to the compulsion of solar force to discharge itself far from itself; the solar outlay without profit is ostentatious. This spectacular consummation of wealth without end, without utility, without recompense and without gratitude is the objective form of glory.

In the furious solar drive to expend its force outside of itself, the void becomes spectacular, matter crystallizes and combines, heliotropic life forms and contracts order. It would be an illegitimate extrapolation of the laws of the special economics of reasonable animals to suppose that these formations are the goal of all this dissipating energy. The solar energy constitutes all the force with which these formations subsist; its essence is in all of them. The exploding force seems to be captured, capitalized in them, but that is only an appearance, of brief duration. The tide of solar energy cannot be arrested; all these systems are destined to be consumed in their turn by the force within them, which will continue the inexorable solar expenditure at a loss. They then are not terminal entities, subsistent causes or goals, whose value would lie in their being, their coherent and self-conserving presence. They are the spectacular and glorious modes in which an unproductive excess is consumed.

On the cold embers of our drifting planet atoms combine, forming crystalline and colloidal aggregates. Colloidal assemblages collect to compose plants, animals, men, each of which draws resources into itself and closes in upon its individuation. Animals may assemble, and men group in social orders, which circulate affluence within themselves. They are greedy for force. Yet they are nostalgic for glory.

For a living organism is a physical and chemical system organized to generate excess force which has to be spent. Because of that excess an organism is characterized by growth and, when growth of the system exceeds manageable limits, propagation. This production of excess is evident already in the simplest organisms; a single piece of lemma will multiply to fill the whole pond. As long as this excess can be dispersed by scissiparity, death is not invented; it is not necessary to the essence of life. Sexless organisms which reproduce by schizogenesis are immortal, continually releasing forces by agitation and division. But the continued pressure of this immortal life results in the formation of more and more complex organisms to consume the excess produced by antecedent ones. They ensure the consumption of life, and themselves die. The more and more spectacular configurations of life—and our life, which, according the Heidegger, is *Dasein,* the locus about which all being becomes an apparition—are essentially *Zum-Tode-Sein,* destined, by their own essence, to die. In their mortality life becomes spectacular. The lucidity produced in the highest formations of life does not only serve for self-conservation. This lucidity of anxious foresight is not produced without the compulsive force of the solar nostalgia for glory.

It is visible in the compulsion to dream, that is, to generate visions that nature in the unending proliferation of its forms cannot concoct; it is visible in the compulsion to intoxication, that it, to the superfluous and unproductive intensification of energy. These compulsions are not incidences of malfunctioning and breakdown in life; they are the force of life itself, which cannot be equated with the series of adjustments to external disturbances by which a system may maintain its equilibrium.

It is visible in the construction of monuments and the cults and in the frenzied waste and the wars, the games, especially those involving competition and gambling, where ruin of health, status and fortune are at stake, the high noon dreams fixed plastically in visual arts and the nonteleological periodicity of music and dance, and the voluptuousness of perverse sexual activity, that detoured from genital and reproductive finality—the unproductive expenditures for which the resources of an immensely burdensome social order are squandered, and which contradict and at times ruin the productive and conservational values of the special economy of reason. In an exceptionally bountiful nature such as is found on the island of Bali, where the very ideas of the production and conservation of wealth are barely developed, it is visible in the extravagant ceremonies of cremation, which constitute the high point and most festive moment of Balinese social existence. In the damp caves where our naked ancestors first herded together, it is visible in the jewelry, inert stones whose dazzle covers over a zero utility, and whose constitution as jewelry is measured by the sacrifice of fortunes. The synthetic jewelry produced by the parsimonious and industrially productive economic systems of recent times, while indiscernible as to beauty and splendor, could never, like real jewels, vain in both senses of the word, function to bear the charge of sexual perversity which requires sumptuous and ostentatious prodigality.

The Kris

Real jewels encrust the handle of the kris dagger, but its magic is invested in the blade. The blade is forged out of iron and lead extracted from meteors hurled upon the sleeping volcanos of Bali by the god Surya the sun. A Balinese must know four languages, for each caste must be addressed in its own language, but the forgers of the kris, although Wesia craftsmen, must be addressed in the language elaborated out of Sanscrit with which the Brahmana priests themselves are addressed. When the radjas of Bali marry, they do not present themselves in person to the girl and before the priest but present their kris; the girl is wed to the solar dagger.

In the morning of the world. Jawaharlal Nehru had called it that, thinking that on the bounteous island of Bali the idea of men seizing nature by the throat had not yet arisen; the Balinese have not imagined vivisecting this island into segments to be allotted to each one for private consumption. They suppose that Bali, which emerged out of the equatorial seas by volcanic explosions, is owned and populated by munificent gods. When Balinese die and are— joyously—cremated, it is to be liberated from the worn flesh so as to be reincarnated again—on Bali. The Balinese dawn rituals, dramas, music, sculpture and poetry struck Nehru, as all visitors, with marvel. In the southern world where the immense majority subsist in aching material craving on more and more devastated continents, Bali flourishes in her dreams and dances.

What has preserved the morning of the world from the noonday devils? In the fifteenth century the Lombok Strait, which separates Bali from the next island, and separates Asia from Australia (on the one side there are cobras, peafowl and tigers in Bali, Java, Sumatra; on the other side there are kangaroos and cockatoos in Lombok and the Flores); it separated Hindu Bali from the Islam that flooded over the rest of Indonesia. Economic unexploitability, in the sixteenth century, kept away the Dutch, who savagely despoiled the resources and communities of Java and the Celebes. Bali is not a spice island, and those tropical fruits ripening on her volcanic slopes would not keep long enough to fatten the burghers of Rotterdam. They left Bali alone. Colonialism was a method of enriching Europe; the Dutch had no interest in the art of governance, which they left in the hands of the radjas, from whom they could exact levies.

But Dutch empire, like a cheese-fed belly, tended to swell. In 1904 a small Chinese merchant steamer was shipwrecked off Sanur, in south Bali. The Balinese are not a sea-going people; their tendency, that of Bali's volcanic essence, is upward. They found the deep sea about their island occupied by sharks and venomous sea snakes, and respected the portents of its nether spirits. Even the few Balinese fishermen there are do not know how to swim; if they capsize, they resign their spirits to the will of the deep. They do not set out to comb the sea of its riches; what the sea ejects upon the shores they will accept of it. They received in this spirit the wreckage of the Chinese boat, lacking the concept of it belonging to someone. But the Chinese had different ideas, and appealed for compensation from the Dutch, under whose protection he was sailing. The Dutch authorities ordered reimbursement from the radja of Badung, whose people had looted white man's property. A move required no doubt not by the indignation but by the idleness of the regent and his troops.

Anak Agung Madé, radja of Badung, received the Dutch emissaries with festivities and a night of dance, but refused their levies. The Dutch came again to demand indemnification plus interests, and costs. The radja refused. The Dutch outfitted the fleet and set up a blockade of the territories of the seven radjas of south Bali. The Chinese merchant community living in Denpasar proposed to pay the reparations demanded for the radja; they valued their cordial relationship with their Balinese customers and their commerce. The radja declined the offer; he himself had gold enough. The Dutch issued an ultimatum. They then proceeded to land troops, armed with twentieth century weaponry; the Balinese guard at Sanur were massacred. From the sea the Dutch ships began to shell the dependencies of Denpasar. That night Anak Agung Madé assembled his people from the rice terraces and the villages and explained to them the military situation and his own resolution, released them from all civic obligations and said to them that each must follow the way of his own honor. The following day the Dutch troops had reached Badung and were closing in, not, as caste Satryas would, assembling before the main gates. The priests and Satryas of the court set fire to all the temples and the palace. The radja, his wives and children and court, his priests and his Satryas, and some 3,600 of his people dressed in white ceremonial robes, covered themselves with all their jewels, and emerged from the flaming palace gates armed only with their celestial kris daggers, and, chanting mantras, advanced directly into the exploding sun and the Dutch firing line. The Dutch guns fired, reloaded and fired, until the last kris bearer was exterminated.

In the following days the last of the noble houses of Pemetjutan, Tabanan and Klungkung came to an end in the same way.

The Rangda

In a village in Bali where a malaise has for some time now been making itself felt, a *balian* falls into a trance and announces it is time to take out the mask of the Rangda, which is kept in the Pura Dalem, the temple of Death.

What does the Rangda mask? Our ideas about reality and symbolism make us determine first that the Rangda is identifiable with a certain historical Javanese queen, Mahendradatta, whose son, Erlangga, was the Balinese prince who became king in Java in A.D.1019. She was said to have been exiled from the court, taken refuge in the forest and taken up the practice of black magic, which in Bali means Tantric Buddhism; what we call the practitioners of white magic are worshippers of the Vedic Shiva. We can see then in the Rangda a figure in the conflict between the Javanese and Balinese social and political orders. Yet the Rangda is religiously identified with Durga the Inaccessible, dark side of the spouse of Shiva. The Rangda is ritually in conflict with the Barong, a lionlike beast, danced by two dancers, who formerly was released at the end of the monsoon by the dragon of the island of Nusa Penida, spreading evil spells and fevers, but with whom at a certain point of their history the Balinese people managed to ally themselves. Comparative ethnology relates the Balinese Barong with the dragon masks of Chinese and Japanese Buddhism. Yet it is when trafficking in black magic is suspected in the village that the Barong comes to dance, to clear space, and in particular to clear space of the black Tantric demons. The Rangda is a female fiend, the Barong a male beast; psychoanalytically oriented anthropologists can see in the Barong a father image, and in the Rangda the image of the teasing, unsatisfying mother, and in the convulsive seizures her dance provokes a repetition of infantile tantrums. Yet the Rangda mask is always donned by a man.

But perhaps we should also have to learn the sense of the Rangda as the Balinese do; we should have to go out into the night until we hear drums, cymbals and gongs of some village assembling for ritual. We shall see the white clad pemangku intoning a mantra and lighting a torch in the courtyard and slitting the throat of a gamecock; it is dark and perhaps raining listlessly and there are stone demons watching in the shadows. The pemangku is assembling power to protect the dancers in the spells they will be subject to, when the masks are taken out of the temple tabernacle and donned. Men are assembling, fifty or a hundred, the whole village, they amass in a circle, seated in lotus position. The torch flickers over their bare brown skin, they become a nameless single organism of rolling heads, tautening arms, shaking torsos. Magical incantations circulate, strident and insistent; men begin to turn into gongs, cymbals, insects, demons. From time to time hoarse cries, like the voices of men thousands of years old, are heard.

After an hour or two gods will materialize in their midst, with emotionless faces, dressed in gold and silver threaded silks, their heads crowned with orchids and sticks of smouldering incense, their trembling fingers continually forming mudras. (In Balinese temple compounds there are demonic figures of all kinds, guarding the gates and corners, but when we enter we find only altars empty as the skies; the gods will never be visible except here, in this trance.) Other creatures will appear in the midst of the mass of uninterruptedly chanting villagers, beasts and demons howling through grimacing masks. For human beings never dance in Balinese dances;

they are represented only as a pair of clowns who turn up from time to time to translate into vulgar language the sacred Kawi language the gods speak. The drama proceeds by metamorphoses, demon into priest into seductress into ape into queen into hog, as though we are in some Nietzschean world where behind every mask there are only more masks. The plot of the ritual drama gets ever more complicated in this media mix of mime, grand opera, farce, high mass, and psychodrama. Cosmic assaults, horrible, ludicrous or obscene, will reenact themselves in the stormy mass of bodies. Finally black and white magic alone in confrontation: the Barong, danced by two dancers entranced, and the fiend Rangda. What resolution could be possible? Rangda dances her screaming curses; she is not vanquished, in the courtyard of the temple of Death those nights, or anywhere else in Bali or in life. Suddenly the Barong, ally of the villagers, vanishes; a dozen men of the village leap up, their fists are closed about their kris daggers made from metals come from the outer darknesses. They are certainly in a deep and strange trance; their eyes are closed, they are moaning, they advance like fidgety automatons toward the leaping Rangda. As they close in she throws a white cloth over her face and abruptly disappears; the men are left thrashing about in the temple court, and before our aghast eyes begin to stab themselves, in the chest, in the mouth, in the jaws, in the forehead, or leap upon their daggers upheld like a phallus between their thighs. Their muscles, agonists and antagonists, are locked in equal tension, and hold the point of the dagger, which draws no blood. They are being watched by the pemangku and his assistants who will rush up and forcibly disarm anyone of them whose trance seems to be lifting lest he kill himself. When the rage subsides some are unconscious, others locked in paralytic seizure, one or another will seize a live gamecock and chew off its head. The pemangku passes among them, pouring holy water and mantras over them, they are dragged to the Barong who has returned and held in his long beard. One after another they awaken, these men of the village, looking a little dazed, a little embarrassed, and disperse quietly in the night.

Excesses

For a General Economy of Trance

What can be more frightful than to see this sudden collapse of personal and physical cohesion, these young men going bezerk in front of our eyes, goring themselves with daggers? We were sitting among them, in this community we now see has willfully set up a situation in which some if its strong young men will break down demented, that arms them for this raging violence whose objective is removed and invincible. They watch, even the children are brought there, and they laugh, entranced or demented themselves, happy, never happier, with a happiness beyond the pleasure their uninhibited everyday sensuality brings flush to their faces, beyond the contentment the extraordinary ecological situation and the bountiful fertility of their island gives them, happy with an inhuman happiness, perhaps that Nietzsche invoked, "a God's happiness, full of power and love, full of tears and laughter, a happiness which, like the sun in the evening, continually gives of its inexhaustible riches and empties into the sea—and like the sun, too, feels itself richest when even the poorest fisherman rows with golden oars!"[2]

But we, rational animals, shudder and look at one another knowingly. With harsh and lucid realism this culture has, by artifice, by theater, materialized the phantasm of evil, and sent forth its strongest and best virility to test the invincibility of this phantasm which perhaps masks but masks, and then this rage, having no resolution, turns on itself. For our part, we know such productions, from Freud's analysis of madness in individuals, from Nietzsche's genealogy of rancor in moral culture.

Our fear adumbrates our judgment, which is negative—that we have witnessed the moment of breakdown, of man's nature, of his culture. More exactly, the breakdown built into the culture, that the culture is built up in order to produce. We divine an essential line of opposition between a historical and productive society, and a ritual-obsessive social and cultural system that is set up and maintained in order to issue in this hysterical defeatism. What, in human affairs, could be more bizarre than a social order where in every village the ideological and representational content of the culture is constituted in trance rituals, where the real decisions of individual and social existence, from medicine prescribed for disease to the decisions which in rational societies accrue to pragmatic information and political savoir-faire, are made by utterances of mediums, random individuals in hysteric seizures?

Madness, or infantilism. When Bateson and Mead take the Rangda figure ethnologically to depict a fertility goddess, and psychoanalytically the teasing and denying mother, and the trance seizure as a tantrum, they are taking the culminating cultural representations and ceremonial of this society as a sublimated route to return to the infantile.

How plausible this is, how familiar such regressive sublimations are to us, we watchers of television! We listen or read on, we are almost persuaded. Then we remember where we are, not in Vienna or in Munich or in Detroit, but in Bali, in a village devoted to rice terracing volcanic slopes, where the most intricate socialization is necessary to ensure that every terrace wall be continually maintained, for they are only made of mud and leak after every rain, to ensure that the water that has to be continuously supplied from the crater lake of the Batur volcano be, as it has been for centuries, distributed to hundreds of autonomous villages above and below this one. These are not primitives picking bananas off trees, but men and women of a pragmatic intelligence and social skills the equivalent of any human society one could choose. We remember that we have been watching the ritual in which the culture has pushed the intellectualization and formalization of itself to an extreme, to a sort of total serialization, where, as Artaud observed, "these mechanically rolling eyes, pouting lips, and muscular spasms produce methodically calculated effects which forbid any recourse to spontaneous improvisation, these horizontally moving heads seem to glide from one shoulder to the other as if on rollers; everything that might correspond to immediate psychological necessities corresponds as well to a sort of spiritual architecture, created out of gesture and mime but also out of the evocative power of a system, the musical quality of a physical movement, the parallel and admirably fused harmony of a tone."[3] And when we look at the cognitive and aesthetic products of the culture, its linguistics, its mathematical and grammatical codifications, its architecture, sculpture and painting, even today in flourishing vitality, its dance, theater and music (in what other society does every village maintain a full orchestra trained in systems of musical composition of a complexity that astonished and influenced Debussy, and which today shows no traces of contamination with the now universal Western music?), when we come finally to acquaint ourselves with this culture's logical systems, its theoretical and philosophical speculations, shall we not perhaps be inclined to ascribe the suggestion that this culture is hysterical or infantile not to scientific positivism but to racism?

Yet how can we deny what we have seen in front of us: this outbreak of crazed violence, turned against itself? Jane Belo, in her empirical study *Trance in Bali*,[4] reports that the battery of tests elaborated by Landis and Bolles at the New York Psychiatric Institute for testing schizophrenics administered by Dr. van Wolfften Palthe to a group of Balinese strongly susceptible to such trances and to a control group of Balinese impervious to trance revealed no significant differences between the groups. "It does not matter what kind of 'abnormality' we choose for illustration," Ruth Benedict wrote, "those which indicate extreme instability, or those which are more in the nature of character traits like sadism or delusions of grandeur or of persecution, there are well-described cultures in which these abnormals function with ease and with honor, and apparently without danger or difficulty to the society."[5]

Shall we then, with Georges Devereux,[6] differentiate between psychoses in which the contradictions that erupt are seated in idiosyncratic traumas, and dissociated states, ethnic psychoses, which eruct unavowable contradictions located in the unconscious segment of the ethnic personality, and which the culture contrives to invest with social recognition because they have a utility for it? Do we not have to appraise a peculiar employment of these psychotic seizures of the culture itself? The ideological and ritual elaboration of character derangements such as extreme instability, sadism, or megalomaniac paranoia would then represent a sort of instinctual work by the culture on its own ethnic psychoses. Could it be that this sort of elaboration of the psychotic seizures of the ethnic personality would leave the individual personality intact? Or could it be that in these societies this elaboration is the condition for the health of the individual personality? Then, with Belo, we would conclude that, individually, "the scheduled seizures they experienced, integrated with the religious life, given a meaning and the dignity of socially significant behavior, may well have served as therapy."[7] We would then surmise that a social elaboration of certain deranged states makes possible an exceptionally consistent constitution of other, orderly and ordering, states in an economy of the ethnic personality whose precise laws are yet to be formulated. The ritual-obsessive and mythical-theatrical elaboration of trance and catelepsy in Bali may then be what makes possible the very exceptional pragmatic discipline and social integration characteristic of this society.

Would not such a conception be what is required by the program of enlightenment? Enlightenment in our time, whose task, as Merleau-Ponty formulated it,[8] is, in political science, in ethics, in psychoanalytic theory, to integrate the irrational into a more comprehensive reason.

Or would this kind of positive assessment of ritual hysteria in Balinese high culture be not only defective, as a schema of comprehensive understanding, but an integral part of an enterprise of destruction of any such culture?

For, Artaud wrote, "this purely popular and not sacred theater gives us an extraordinary idea of the intellectual level of a people who take as the basis of their civic festivals the struggles of a soul prey to the larvae and phantoms of the beyond."[9] Artaud saw in it pure theater, as opposed to Western, that is, psychological theater, and wrote, "What vitiates Western theater [and Western practice?] is that it is concerned with man while the Oriental theater is concerned with the universe."[10]

Our fear for man interprets as demented collapse the kris dancer who throws himself to the trance point where self-destructive ferocity and invincibility, immolation and glory, the meteors enflammed by the sun and the life armed with the kris are one.

Our speculative theory makes psychological theater out of the speculative spectacle. And explains it in function of its—or our—economics. In function of the special economy of closed systems, such as finite, insular, humankind, insular and nonhistorical cultures. It makes an exorcism or a catharsis out of a theater made, Artaud said, "to collectively lance the abscess,"[11] to invoke the cosmic compulsions which lie beneath our morality, our taboos, our institutions, to detonate in incredible images forces destructive of the special economy of closed systems of circulation. Pure theater effects a systematic depersonalization of feelings and psychological states, transforms them into diagrams, hieroglyphics of metaphysical compulsions, which, far from exorcising, it renders spectacular.

Theatrical pleasure, the pleasure in mask and costume and disguise, pleasure of transvestitism, was subjected to analysis by Nietzsche. For him the specifically theatrical pathos consists not, as in the classical interpretation of Greek tragedy as truth-drama, in watching the resolution of a situation of pure appearance, watching the unmasking, but in the masking itself, impotent transformation of the forms, pleasure in disguise and masquerade. The pleasure, pure superficiality, is deep, is metaphysical. For before our affliction, the pain that is in our existence—and which is, finally, our mortality—theoretical or optimist culture promises a cure, postponing the end, elaborating either a mythical immortality, or accomplishing a real immortality by culture itself, that is, an immortality in works and spiritual achievements. But this enterprise of theoretical consolation is an illusory fixation of forms to cover over the uncontainable forces of universal transience. Theatrical or tragic culture is contrived to bring about inward union with the universal will. The consolation it gives, the sole veridical consolation, is to find enkindled in one's heart the pleasure which is that of the universal substance—not a contentment in the stabilization of forms, in immortality, but an exaltation in the ceaseless formation and transformation of forms. In this ecstasy alone there is reconciliation with the imminent destruction of our own form. Nietzsche takes theater to be religion, where the reconciliation that makes beings doomed to annihilation able to take up their transitory existence, and the only genuine redemption, is realized.

This theater is true, not with the kind of truth that theoretical representations claim, a conformity between the forms produced by the theoretical mind and the forms produced by the world-play, but rather with a transcendental truth, a conformity of the form-producing mind, which recognizes now that all its formations are false, with the form-producing expenditure of universal force. The epiphany of this truth would determine the supreme rituals and the decisive action of a culture radically opposed to theoretical culture.

But is not the Nietzschean metaphysics in its own way a psychology of theater? Transcendental and no longer empirical psychology, to be sure. For now what is captivating in theater is not the exhibition of psychological states and their conflicts, but the transformation of the representational subjectivity. This transformation does not consist in an *emendatio mentis* that would lead to truthfulness; in fact everything in theater is fantasy and phantasm, and false. It consists in recognizing that as the locus of a production of phantasms, of inconsistent forms, theater joins with the ultimate will in Being itself, which indefatigably engenders forms and remorselessly effaces them. It is just this conformity that is consoling, healing, redeeming. That is the serious and deep consolation: consolation for the pain that is our own, our mortality.

But as soon as we have seen that, do we not recognize that the Nietzschean metaphysics of theater is also an economics? And a special economics? As though there were an irreducible force or will in life that needed to be consoled, that needed to be recompensed for its pain, that needed to be healed psychologically before it is really, nonetheless, annihilated. But would not the laws of pure or universal theater be the laws of general economics? Does not the theater belong to the night, to its empty celestial spaces where solar energies are squandered without recompense?

There are theories that come too late, and miss their chance to have been true for awhile. There are also theories that come too early, and have to wait awhile to be true. Ten years ago they built the Bali Beach Hotel and the airport, and the island paradise of the bare-breasted women got a place on the map of world, that is, Western, economy. Soon the entranced will be recompensed for their show; they will become actors and the children of the sun will perform in limelight. Last year, in Ubud, a ruined radja, concerned about finding the funds for the spectacular cremation of his father his station demanded, sold the rights to American television. And they have rebuilt the palace of Anak Agung Madé, the radja of Badung; its pavilions are rented out to tourists.

Notes

1. Friedrich Nietzsche, *Nachgelassene Schriften 1870-1973, Nietzsche Werke, Kritische Gesamtausgabe*, ed. Giorgio Colli & Mazzino Montinari, Vol. 3, Part 2, (Berlin and New York: de Gruyter, 1973), pp. 253-254.
2. Friedrich Nietzsche, *Joyful Wisdom*, trans. Thomas Common (New York: Ungar, 1960), § 337.
3. Antonin Artaud, *The Theater and Its Double*, trans. Mary Caroline Richards (New York: Grove, 1958), p. 55.
4. Jane Belo, *Trance in Bali* (New York: Columbia Univ. Press, 1960), p. 10.
5. Ruth Benedict, "Anthropology and the Abnormal," *Journal of General Psychology*, 10 (1934): 59-60.
6. Georges Devereux, "Normal and Abnormal; the Key Problem of Psychiatric Anthropology," in *Some Uses of Anthropology* (Washington, D.C.: The Anthropological Society of Washington, 1956), pp. 23-48.
7. Belo (above, note 4), p. 9.
8. Maurice Merleau-Ponty, *Sense and Non-Sense*, trans. Hubert and Patricia Dreyfus (Evanston, Ill.: Northwestern Univ. Press, 1964), p. 3.
9. Note found on the manuscript for "La métaphysique et la mise en scéne," *Oeuvres complètes* (Paris: Gallimard, 1964), Vol. IV, p. 288.
10. *The Theater and Its Double*, p. 31.

Black Gods

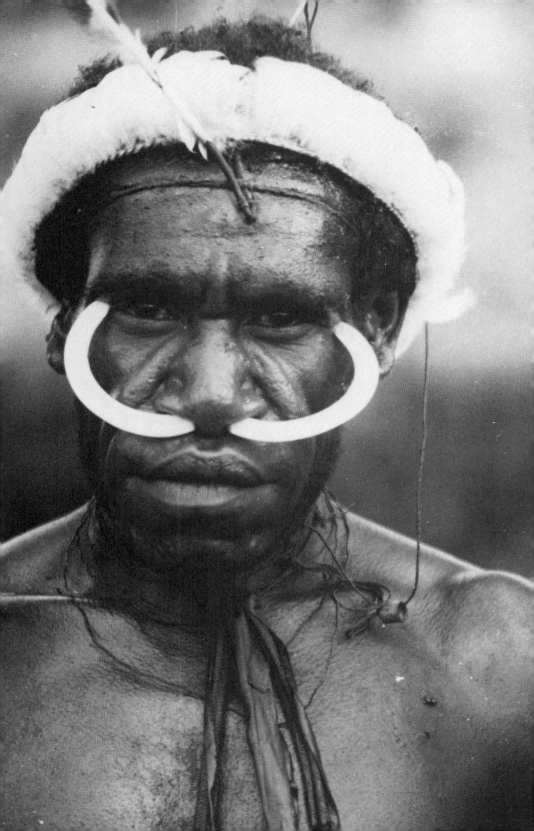

WAR PARTY IN IRIAN JAYA. FIFTEEN-FOOT LANCES, SPRINGING skyward over the leaping bodies of headhunters. The birds glitter like flying sparks in their wake, the jungle quivers more intense about its most spectacular issue. Black torsos gleaming with pig grease; scarlet, orange, blue zigzagging across the foreheads and pumping chests. Heads crowned with sprays of flickering and whipping bird-of-paradise plumes. Clad with nothing but the holims holding the penises in arm-long erections, making the bodies only the more naked. The hills and the gorges shouting with the cascading war-cries. Naked outbreak, shouting arrogance, challenge, insult, provocation, boasting, ostentation, monstrous demonstration.

Where is the pride in, or even the sense of, being human in all this? Out to hunt members of their own species. The bodies plucked of their natural down and greased with the fat of butchered pigs, the heads' dense kinky hair used to feather them with the tails of dead birds. Tusks of boars fiercely projecting from the punctured noses. Testicles of boars or of tree kangaroos tied to the arms. Their own penises prolonged into two or three foot erections by gourds tied to the testicles. What is this grotesque super-prick supposed to proclaim—aggressive arrogant power to fertilize the jungle with the human species? Or is it not rather that the human species is here as it were still at the beginning stages, when it had no clear idea of what it was, and was being deviated monstrously into a collage of fiercer, gigantic, more destructive bestial shapes? The penis turned not so much into a swollen organ of fecundating sperm as into a hard and dry pointed tusk, as though not an organ for the affirmation of the human species but for its destruction, not a gland to fertilize the ovaries in females but a horn to eviscerate one's fellows.

Night now. I have been tolerated, or admitted, in the men's house. They are all here, those who had gone to their wives' houses, perhaps even copulated, are back now, greased bodies vaguely entwined as they stir and sleep in the mosquito-repelling smoke. Wearing the holim still, as though among men now the penis is not an organ of male bonding and pleasure either. They sleep fitfully, the stirrings and turnings communicated down the line. I am left to lie apart. How hard it is to sleep. Not because of the rude floor, the smoke; I have often enough camped here and elsewhere. Because of them: what common pact, what law, what sense of common humanity can I count on to entrust myself to sleep in this house full of frightful carvings of stiff and leering spirits, this house built on bamboo poles under each of which there was first planted a human skull, this house full of cannibals? Did I sleep? Did I have nightmares of monsters—or did I lie sleepless all the night and see the monsters in the Stone Age night of Jewika in Irian Jaya?

Males, bearing an arm-long hard and erected penis by day as well as by night, in twenty-four hour tumescence. Is this the purest and most extreme form of phallic culture? Yet it does not seem to be the most sexed form of culture: they rather have a horror over the loss of secretions in intercourse and indulge in it only occasionally, and briefly; they marry late and have but two children, abstaining the five years that the woman nurses the first child, and from then on after the birth of the second child. Among men, homosexuality and masturbation are shunned with the same horror over loss of secretions. What is in those huge penis sheaths they never take off, even to sleep, among men in the men's house? The suspicion arises, are they in fact castrated? Surely not; but, running off to war with penis erected and flailing the air in front of them, are they not the visible exhibition of the castration eventuality? Rather than competition of pawing and lusty bulls, is not the combat of these phallic males castration? And is not this the very meaning of their monstrous and headhunting society? Headhunting—a permanent state of hostility of each compound against the next—is not among them an extreme form of conflict resolution in society; rather the agrarian and food-hunting association, that of women, is for the sake of the headhunting. In a deep sense their society is headhunting; the tendency is for the males to do nothing but that. Headhunting, not war for the sake of territory, for the sake of taking over more land to garden, for no territory is annexed; not war for the sake of booty, for the enemy compound is not plundered, or not plundered of anything but the heads of its males; not war for the sake of conquest, for the enemy is not enslaved, but cannibalized. Society for the sake of headhunting, then, for it is as companions of battle alone that these men are associated.

For Freudian psychoanalysis human society is founded on the castration complex: the prohibition of immediate gratification is the first law of civilization. From the interdiction of a field of immediate pleasure objects there is elaborated systems of implements, economic commodities, markets, political identities, aesthetic and ritual objects, linguistic constructions, which do not give immediate gratification but offer significance. Objects have become significant, pleasure-surfaces have given place to signs. Psychoanalytic interpretation consists in finding phallic significance in tools, artworks, cognitive entities, sacramental objects. The first pleasure object to become significant, through the prohibition of immediate gratification, was the object immediately on hand, one's own body; the castrated penis became a phallus.

The phallus does not acquire its original fetishist significance from being the most salient element in real sexual copulation, nor from being an imaginary element, image of the invisible vital flow transmitted in generation, nor from being the most symbolic element in copulation, apt to symbolize the copula in the logical order. The phallus is first constituted in repression; it is that which was first discovered as a lack, a want of being. This lack opens the space beyond the immediately given into which signs signify. The objects that have become signs, that do not offer immediate gratification but refer beyond themselves, refer clandestinely to this absence. The objects open to civilized, that is, castrated, man are metaphors and metonymies of the phallus.

Lévi-Strauss had proposed to elucidate elements like the Polynesian *mana* by their structural function in the field of signs.[1] Terms whose signification is not circumscribed by opposition to other significations, they figure as "floating signifiers." Their occurrence, and even necessity, can be understood by the modern structuralist treatment of cultural orders as semiotic systems. It has shown that the field of significations is not extended additively term by term, each new signifier introduced to signify a new signification discovered or constituted. Rather with the first sign-system, the whole universe becomes significant, all signification is there, and the most rudimentary language, that of the ooo-aah, *Fort-Da* language of Freud's grandchild,[2] is capable of signifying anything that has to be signified. The new signifiers that are introduced do not extend the field of what can be signified, but rather make new discriminations within it. There is, then, always a surplus of the signifiable over and beyond what has been discriminated by signs, and a floating signifier in each semiotic system functions to mark this excess.

Lacan identifies the phallus not as such a floating signifier in the sense that the phallus would be a sign whose signification would be constantly shifting in the system. The phallus is rather the original lack in the system. It has been barred from the first. It is what is always signified by metaphor and by metonymy. It is the zero-signifier that is lacking from the first, and whose lack causes the shifting in the field of signifiers, the combinations and the substitutions, the metonymies and the metaphors, in the speech addressed to the other.[3]

And the first signifier of the phallus, the first phallic metaphor, in the speech addressed by the infant to the other, is the infant himself.

In civilization man is a fabricator of signs because a man is a sign. Within civilization an infant is significant before he is. Before he was born, perhaps before he was even conceived, the infant already figured in the parental discourse. What functioned as the material substrate of the signifier of the infant in the parental discourse was not the real fetus but an image, the "imaged body" of the infant, imagined especially by the mother. The doubling up was possible first because the real fetus is invisible and its presence known by the mother only partially, through stirrings, movements, kickings, a fragmented body, fragmented not only in space but across time. There was an urgent vital reason to produce this imaginary body. It is what will enable the mother to not live through the childbearing as a fragmentation of her body, a dismembering, a loss of part of her own substance, or a threat to her whole existence. The production of the "imaged body" of the infant is the means by which she overcomes the anxiety of the imago of the body in fragments—her own.

Once born the infant lives through contact with the maternal substance. This state of dependence, of parasitism, involves the eventuality of there not being total and continual satisfaction of its needs, and the infant knows anxiety. Non-satisfaction is due mainly to the whims of the other, the mother. This arbitrariness gives rise in the infant to phantasms of omnipotence. The original omnipotence is that of the other, of the mother—not the infant himself. The infantile energies are torn between appetite and demand—between relationship with the complements of need supplied by the other and the relationship with the other, in the form of a demand for love, a demand for the pure gift of total satisfaction. The infant cries between the particularity of the need satisfied or not, and the totality of the demand for love. It is given the bottle and put to sleep. The satisfaction of need in a particular moment functions as a refusal of the demand for love, which, however, does not cease being formulated in the sleeping organism.[4] The terms of every language are formulated to mark the place of the absence of objects, and are themselves formed by the unreality of the objects; the infantile language, or more exactly the inscription, the hieroglyphics and the rebus, of the infantile dream continues to formulate only the demand still addressed to the other.

Civilization is equipped with reflection. A mirror offers a child a representation of himself, at a distance. The mirror image is recognized by an infant beginning at the age of six months, an achievement which the higher apes seemingly never attain, but an achievement which they do not have the same kind of biological interest in attaining, and which Lacan has explained.[5] For a human infant lives in a state of corporeal fragmentation, as though born premature, unable to coordinate neurologically and without motor integration, existing in dependence and anxiety. In this situation the identification of the mirror image as himself is not merely a predicative and judgmental synthesis, "That is me!"; it is an affective and projective identification. Not an identification of it, but an identification with it. The infant is alienated into the image, captivated by it. For the mirror image functions vitally as a factor of integration: it presents the infant with an anticipated composition of the fragments of his body into a subsistent totality. It presents the infant with an ideal version of himself. In pleasure the infant identifies with this ego ideal. The stage of fascination with the mirror image is also the stage of the original narcissism. For it is also a suicide, a losing oneself in the stagnant element of the image. The infant is alienated from the Heraclitean flux of his own experience of himself and of his environment, to identify himself with this mirror object posited as a distance, fixed, identical and substantial.

There is already something of a linguistic structure in this identification. For from now on there is a material element—the mirror image—which can be referred to, by the child and by others, as the signifier of the subject. This signifier can be set forth, displayed, paraded about, presented to others; it can discourse with others. It has a metonymic form: a signifier for a part of the child (the future totality) has been substituted for the actual and present reality, the physiological and experiential reality of the infant, which had no signifier.

With this metonymic signifier the child himself enters into the discourse in which he had already figured. The imaged body that figured in the parental discourse to signify him before he was born he can now identify, project himself into, make it speak. Make it bear his demand to the other.

But once the child enters into the parental discourse he finds himself subject to its law. The paternal law requires that the infant detach himself definitively from his physical reality as a pleasure object, to identify himself with the signifier that bears him into discourse. The law requires that the child's own body as a pleasure object be taken out of his hands, requires renunciation of masturbation, requires castration.

The law is the word of the father. The father intervenes to counter the phantasm of maternal omnipotence with the potency of his authority. The authority of the father is the authority of his word. It is not equivalent to a real fear effectively produced. Subjection to the word of the father is not equivalent to the maintenance of a real threat of castration whose reproduction in memory would produce the inhibiting fear.

To see this, one would have to recognize, with contemporary philosophies of language, that speech acts are not only representations, representing an ordered reality. Speech is not only indicative but also imperative; speech itself orders. The outcome of the Oedipus complex will be that the demand put to the other will be diversified, multiplied, articulated in the ways of language, of symbolism, of culture. The infantile libido is not suppressed, abolished, by a real castration threat; it is deviated, extended, formulated. The word of the father is not to be reduced to the physical reproduction of a gesture that produces fear; it is the word of law, the first instance of the ordering, ordaining word.

The paternal word will be taken seriously when the infant discovers the castration of the mother. Melanie Klein reported that the infant, who has no perception of the vagina as the recipient of genital penetration and thereby itself a pleasure object, originally perceives the mother as containing a penis within the fragmented imago of her body that forms in the infantile consciousness. Castration phobia in boys and penis envy in girls does not originate in real threats of castration addressed to the child by the real father (more often in fact formulated by the mother), but in the discovery that the penis is missing in the mother. Missing at the place from which the child has come to understand he has himself issued. There arises the phallus as what is signified by the desire of the mother, that which is addressed in the voluptuous desire of the mother the infant has felt by feeling it turned in his direction. There arises the voluptuous wish to be a phallus for the mother. In order to be able to demand of her not only the satisfaction of particular needs, but the absolute gift of love.

The seriousness of the word of the father is engraved on the body of the mother, in the castration of the mother. It designates the phallus, pure signification and original absence, as that to which the desire of the mother has always been addressed. If the child can will to subject himself to the law of the father, if he can will the castration of his penis from his body as immediate pleasure-object, this is because he wills to be the absence designated by the craving of the mother, he wills to be the signified which the word of the father designates on the perceptible body of the mother. He invests in the phallic form of his specular ego the libidinous gratification prohibited in his immediate body.

But in appropriating the paternal law, in himself pronouncing upon his own body the law that requires castration, the child puts himself in the place of the father. What wills in him is the desire to identify himself with the phallus the mother lacks, but what speaks in him is the word of the father. The phallic phantasm is henceforth that which is always designated, but passed over in silence, whenever the law of the father speaks in the child. The word and the law, as the child will set them forth, embody them, pronounce them in discourse, are metaphors for the phallus.

The infant and his wants are outcries; the libido that speaks speaks in the name of the father. The libido that is articulated, that has interiorized the law, has taken the place of the father, speaks in the name of the father. The Oedipus crisis is resolved when the child is capable of being a father, reproducing a family, when the voice of his desire legislates castration.

This history is to be sure difficult to formulate. In *Totem and Taboo* Freud elaborated the process of the passage from the state of nature to the state of society or culture by studying the castration complex writ large on the body politic. He tells of the primal father who appropriated to himself all the women as his pleasure objects, and of the sons malevolent and belligerent from being deprived of women. The father was one day murdered by a coalition of the sons, and devoured by them. This murder should issue in free—and fratricidal—competition for the women among the insurgents. But the coalition of the brothers, the negative participation in patricide, becomes, positively, cannibalistic ritual, the eucharist by which each partakes of the body and blood of the murdered father. Cannibalism is originally cannibalization of the father, incorporation, internalization of the father.[6] In this incorporated, internalized form, in this love, this primary homosexuality, he abides, and his force, his law returns. Society in mankind is not then based on the biological brotherhood of men united by their descendancy from a common father, but upon the patricidal brotherhood of men united by mystical communion in the body of the father which they have reincorporated. The original form of law that orders society is the interdiction of free competition for the women as pleasure-objects; the original decree that institutes language—that is, verbal languages, but also those languages which Lévi-Strauss has shown the kinship systems and the economy to be, systems for the circulation of women and of goods, as speech systems are first systems for the circulation of verbal material—the original word that orders language is the incest prohibition. The original spirit world forms not out of a longing for immortality on the part of primitive men, living a life "brutish, mean, and short," and who carry the instinct for self-preservation to the point of excluding death from their consciousness, but rather out of a will to put an end to the elders, which risks their lives and immortalizes the slain. For the guiding spirits of the original society are the cannibalized biological genitors.

Fifty years after Freud, Lacan, surveying the anthropological field work, concludes that this Freudian account is verified by no empirical evidence. It is, he states, a true myth, elaborated by Freud on the basis of individual psychology—the passage of the infant into a libido structured and articulated according to law and driven into a field of objects all of which function as relays for and symbols of a demand put to the other which has been barred, rendered unconscious.[7] One could remark that positive anthropology could never verify, or disallow, the Freudian explanation; anthropology would always find either primates living in nature and as beings of natural desire, or men already living in society and in language, and the passage would elude anthropology, which is itself a science, that is, an operation within the semiotic order. The passage itself could be re-presented now, to us, in culture, only in the form of a myth.

What the Freudian myth is able to teach is that the father that socializes and civilizes is not the physical reality of the father wielding a real threat of castration to separate the sons from the women. Such an "authority" is overcome as it were by biology itself, by the physical maturation of the sons which will inevitably make them the stronger. The father that founds the human social community is the internalized, spiritualized, father. And this forces us to see that the socialization does not bind through a persistence in memory of the image of the real threat of aggression from a more powerful other outside, but through the eucharist by which the paternal reality, now vanquished and abolished, is constituted as an internal imperative that makes the libido speak, that is, address itself to the demand of the other.

Once we recognize that this understanding is the positive yield of the myth, we will be able to understand what the anthropologists in fact find in societies judged primitive—not patricide but head-hunting. In the highlands of Irian, girls are trained in the skills of the adults as they become physically capable of them, but the boys are not really educated at all; they wander freely all day among themselves, without tasks or training in the world of adults. For the boy to become a man is not to become a lesser associate, apprentice, of his father, but to take the place of his father. And man's activity is not economic—the women garden and gather; the men kill. Thus boys become men not through education but through initiation. It is not the place of the real father that is vacated; when his time comes the boy may very well be stronger, more vigorous, with senses keener in the jungle and blood braver than his ageing, deteriorating, perhaps many times wounded real father. The boy seeks out an ideal father, strongest, most spectacular, boldest, whose interdiction is armed. It is this ideal killer, sought on the field on combat, that is brought back and cannibalized, and, internalized, becomes the guiding, ruling spirit of the initiate. Thus psychoanalytic anthropology has made us understand what first struck us as incredible: that the spirit world which holds the Papuan tribes together and that accompanies each warrior through life as his supernatural guide and personal law can be identified as the enemies they have cannibalized.

But has this psychoanalysis accounted for the dark psychology of those gods? The white men come to tell of a God the Father with a white soul, yet psychoanalysis sees their God arisen out of the same patricide and returning in the same eucharist. That is not how the white priests tell it; for them in the beginning was the Word and the Word was with God and the Word was God. The black gods of the jungle are only heard in war-cries. Does psychoanalysis really know that their God and these demons are the same?

I shall not offer an alternative account, or myth, of the deep Freudian teaching that castration is the operation that effects the passage from natural existence to society or to culture, or an alternative account or myth of the father as ego ideal rather than as authority figure, or of cannibalism rather than headhunting as the eucharist of man's social existence. I shall rather essay a speculative elaboration of my opening picture of these individuals, not as a society with primitive simplicity and primitive cohesion, but as a multitude of essentially unsocialized, uncivilized individuals, not yet constituting a human species, spectacular, not recognizing any common humanity, constructed by collage of fiercer, more gigantic, more destructive bestial material—monsters.

The Freudian and Roheimian explanations presuppose that we are here dealing with a primitive society, with the primitive form of society, and that its central social acts, headhunting and cannibalism, are in fact the primitive or essential acts that constitute society. The underlying assumptions—as old as Platonism—are that civilization is constituted out of the prohibition of immediate gratification, but that the libidinal demand put on the other, in its absolute and total character, is not, cannot be suppressed, is rather repressed, deviated, has gone underground, where it has become insatiable and infinite, driving force gone astray in an unending field of symbols. If that is what civilization consists in—the constitution of an ever-extending field of entities that are objects, posited at a distance, and objects of desire, but each of them stricken with an essential absence, each one a metaphor or metonymy for the phallic ideality barred from the start—then indeed what one has to understand is how the castration complex issues in subjection to the order of law.

But let us list features of the Irian highlanders which make questionable whether this explanation of their headhunting and cannibalistic way of life is applicable, and first whether what it sets out to explain even exists among them—namely, civilization.

1. We have here not a libido deviated from the demand for immediate gratification and driven into a never-ending field of symbolic objects of desire; we have an essentially obsessive culture, where the supreme act is the headhunting exploit and the cannibalistic feast itself. One cannot really say that the headhunting feats and the cannibalistic feast—the encounter with the authority figure and with the ego ideal writ large—is the inauguration into adulthood,

language, law, society, civilization; it is for them all that adulthood, culture, society consist in. The rudimentary hunting and gathering, agriculture, craft and art exist for the sake of headhunting and cannibalistic orgies, and not the reverse.

2. Is the headhunting and cannibalism essentially initiation ritual? That is, the act by which the unsocialized youth becomes a man by taking the place of the father, assuming the name of the father, becoming a father? But there is an altogether striking resentment, among them, of paternity. There is a kind of repugnance before generation, its secretions and its weaknesses; the men sleep together in the men's house, even do much of their own cooking, and a husband returns, after intercourse with his wife in her house, to the men's house to sleep. They marry late, shun the physiological commotion in the genitals, sire one child that is then nursed by the woman four or five years, during which time husband and wife practise sexual continency, and then beget a second one, and then cease all sexual intercourse. Among themselves the men do not tolerate homosexuality or even masturbation. Men *are* headhunters; headhunting is neither initiation into, nor ancillary of, an enterprise of production and reproduction.

3. To be sure, the enormous production and expenditure of energy in battle issues in a fabulous production of what combat among animal bands does not give rise to: fantastical and fierce personal decoration, fabulous identifications with birds and beasts of prey both real and invented, a sumptuous artistry of weapons, body movements, war cries, victory orgies and magical consummations of defeat. But all this is, as it were, one unendingly reverberated war-cry; it is not a discourse, that is, the dialectic of mediation and peace. The war-cry is not a sign, that is, an element which acquires its definition and its function only within the semiotic system where it marks a differentiation and a transition. It is rather an irruption, a defiance, an insult, a provocation, a refusal of every response.

4. Combat among them is ceaseless, perhaps going back for hundreds of generations, but the first white patrols were completely perplexed by its character: these people seemed not to have ever been

able to renounce an armed conflict which is gratuitous and futile. It is not war for booty—the enemy encampments are not plundered; combat rather occurs in a no-man's-land between encampments. It is not war for territory—the encampments are seminomadic, subsisting in a kind of slash-and-burn agriculture, and do not fight in order to extend territorial holdings; no form of empire-building seems to have existed among them. It is not war for conquest—slavery and serfdom are unknown. The stealing of women where they are in short supply may well be an occasion to resume combat, but during the fighting women freely pass back and forth along the battle lines picking up arrows without fear of being smitten or captured.

5. In addition combat is individual in a strange way. There are no war-chiefs, no real battle strategy to speak of; in the battle each one is alone, both fighting without orders and seeking only to get an enemy head for himself—not seeking to partake in a joint assault or offensive against a common enemy.

6. The explanation that has been offered to account for these strange features of headhunting is that it is governed by a metaphysical economy of death. Death for them has always a human explanation, and therefore a human resolution. Death among them occurs by open enemy aggression, and what looks to us like death due to disease or natural causes is for them due to witchcraft or poisoning on the part of the other. To deal with death then is to cause a death in the other camp. The strange exigency to preserve an equilibrium, to insist that life cannot be smitten with impunity, forces and expounds a rationalization of death and thus of life. Strange indeed. In this way the death suffered is perhaps compensated for, but not restored, nor rendered positive, except as the element that will inexorably lead to still another loss in one's own camp. The more one admires the prowess of this Stone Age people to devise a culture not preoccupied with piecemeal comforts and securities, but with dealing with, humanizing, death, refusing to suspend all human existence on something inapprehendable like chance or destiny, the more one is baffled by the inefficacy, even the absurdity of their solution. For

they compensate for existence subject to inapprehendable blows of chance by creating an existence of serial and irresolvable terror.

Psychoanalysis shows the original constitution of the sign of man in the infantile project of becoming phallus, in order to be able to demand of the other total love. The Marquis de Sade is one whose fundamental position is marked by hatred of the mother. One can at once suppose that this hatred is not original; that first came the demand for total love. The Sadean libertine would be another figure of the phallic male. Indeed women can be said to figure in his work only as grotesque versions of the phallic mother—or else as pure material for the libertine in his phallic enterprises.

The libertine according to Sade is a lord, an aristocrat, to be sure, but of the most essential kind: a figure of sovereignty. Libertinage is defined formally by its relationship with law. It determines itself to violate the law for the sake of violating the law; thus it has a maxim of its own, and constitutes itself in singularity. Sovereign singularity is constituted by violation of every law of morality and religion, is constituted in criminality by the violation of every form of social pact, in essential sacrilege by the unremitting aggression against God, in essential monstrosity by violation of nature. The sovereign Sadean heroine Clairwill dreams of perpetrating a crime whose consequences would be without end in the universe, such that her deed would prolong itself throughout the universe and throughout all time as a malignant force of disorder. Amélie wishes to die by murder, so that her inevitable death itself would serve as an occasion for crime.

The entire combinatorium of vice is placed by Sade under the sign of Sodom. Through this sign contemporary thought could see Sade's project belonging to the closure of phallocratic normativity. But what does this sign signify? Does it signify? Here the genital organ is bared neither as an instrument to give pleasure to another or to reproduce the species, nor into an autocratic icon of self-activating sufficiency. For sodomy, a concept which belongs not to the rational and normative homosexuality of Athens, but to the black theology of

Baal, is the usage of the male organ as a weapon aimed at the species as such. It is the use of the erect penis to release the germ of the race only it is excreta, and to gore, to disembowel the receiving partner.

Libertine versus Oedipus Rex: the Sadean phantasm depicts a structure essentially different from that of the Freudian myth. Different from the phallic male constituted in castration, which is the interdiction put on immediacy with the other, an interdiction which articulates the sublimation of desire, the deviation of the libido into the continually more diversified and unendingly deferred universe of symbols. The phallic male constituted in sodomy lives out the refusal of the gift of the other to oneself, refusal of subjection to the omnipotent desire of the other, refusal of every demand and every claim of the other. Here the Oedipus complex does not issue in assuming the name of the father, constituting oneself as one that is a phallus and offers oneself in gift to the other and demand put on the other, for the reproduction of the lineage. It rather issues in an act aimed nihilistically at the process of species reproduction and thus at the species as such.

But is not sodomy itself a sign, a symbolic act? Does it not then presuppose a semiotic system, and indeed does it not arise only within a certain state of rational civilization? Is not that even reflected in the fact that the project of integral monstrosity is elaborated not in Sade's life but in his literature?

In truth sodomy is only apparently here a semiotic term in an aberrant discourse. The personages in the House of Sodom are not really phallic and cultivated individuals who, once identified by a sovereign and libertine act, then pursue a certain activity, discourse or destiny; they are without depth, without density, personages of a single act, they are the matricide, the infanticide, the coprophagist, the sodomite, personages whose substance is exhausted in the repetition of their mania. The depravity does not only define the libertine, but exhausts his reality; the libertine has nothing to say, and his existence nothing to promulgate, but this depravity. His existence consists in subsisting until the moment when he can perpetrate his vice. When it is perpetrated it is accompanied not by representational discourse justifying it in terms of some normalized system, some black utopia, but by outbursts of malediction, derision and blasphemy shouted at God, supreme point of convergence of norms. Depravity does not function as a sign to deviate the code of a culture into some other elaboration; it functions to extract the libertine from every code.[8] The sodomite is not an invert living according to the codes of an underground or damned brotherhood; his existence consists in nothing but the pure repetition of a single act, which, disemboweling the other with the natural organ for social bonding and species reproduction, goes each time to the limit of outrage against the normative. If the phallus in a castrated civilization is a floating zero-signifier, we might say that the sodomite phallus is a floating minus-signifier.

Yet does not the existence of the libertine get realized in sovereignly significant acts which have an essential relationship to language? For if the depravity is not to fall back into sociological, psychological, biological or even physico-chemical determinations, and into the generalities of the rational discourse that comprehends pathologies, it must set itself forth as a profession of atheism. Is it not the interpretation elaborated by Sade that constitutes depravity as libertinage? Language, and in particular logically structured language, is the medium of the generic; through its terms, all general, and its arguments, which persuade through their transindividual evidence, logically structured language reproduces and reconstitutes in communicative moves the normative structure of the species in the individual. Does not the outrage, no less than the exemplary act, set itself forth in the field of communication as a sign, and thus presuppose the laws of the equivalence and commutability of signs, and thus the symbolic order and the primacy of species existence? Does not every act that means to bar or repress a symbol, or all symbolism, inevitably get recuperated by the symbolism, get understood and interpreted? Does not a sign have its effect only by persuading, and by persuading does it not always appeal to the primacy of the generic?

Yet one has to see that the depravity is not perpetrated as a sign.

The act is not mediated through generic representations. The debauched consciousness is one in which the inhibitory interposition of generalizing memories or expectations, which, in a state of weariness of impulses can substitute feelings of remorse or of apprehension for the act, have been suppressed; the impulse then issues immediately in the act. It issues in the repetition of an act of consummate depravity, and does not intentionally project a field or series of consequences. In its sodomite essence, it is an act in which communication within the genus, and the genus itself as physical substrate and even physical reality of communication, are liquidated in the individual.

The corruption spreads not through persuasion but through complicity. The acts and the words do not persuade through their sense and their sensibleness, but infect the passionate depths of the mind. All the sophistical elaborations of the libertine reason do not convince, they corrupt. *"La mère en prescrira la lecture à sa fille,"* Sade wrote on the title page of *Philosophy in the Bedroom*. He dreamt of writing a book that could be tolerated by neither the court nor the Commune, by no social order, in no home, a book such that were it but to exist, it would one day be found, and whoever would so much as open it would be lost.

Corruption finds its accomplices—not because the impulse it illustrated would in fact exist also in the law-abiding citizen, the normalized individual. That is, it does not owe its effect to being an element of human nature, and thus only repressed or dissimulated in the rationalized and normalized citizen. Precisely the sodomite depravity liquidates this dimension of the generic and its cogencies. The depravity infects not because of its content but because of its form. It outrages its witness. The outrage means that there is something else in him besides the generic norms he incarnates, and that is outraged even after the sophisms of the libertine have been unmasked and refuted by the common reason in him. This something else is his own latent singularity. This singularity, by virtue of its very existence, however latent, is already an accomplice of the libertine project.

The interpretation of headhunting and cannibalism in terms of the passage from the state of subjection to the natural, biological father to that of subjection to a murdered, incorporated, idealized father is supplied as an explanation for the origin of the spirit world and for the origin of human society governed by law. To construct another explanation it is first necessary to see how headhunting, unlike war, singularizes. Rather than being a common enterprise of defense or expansion of the group and its territory, wealth or numbers, the compound, its division into men's and women's activities, its economic projects, its occupancy of territory exist for the sake of headhunting. In the battle each is seeking out an adversary for himself, not to eliminate but to take on and cannibalize, internalize. In a pitched battle engaging hundreds, most often hardly more than one will fall. The one killed was one isolated in his own ferocity, not, as in modern war, uniformized, killing as an interchangeable figure of the armed force of the enemy State. He was one that appeared emblazoned with the tusks, beaks, plumes of the beasts and birds of prey he alone had the chance or skill to find and kill, singularized now in the figure of his last exultant or foolhardy and mortal leap. The one that has killed that kain is isolated by this stroke of prowess or fate. The core of secrecy and singularity that he now harbors until he finds his own death is occupied by the force of the one he has slain, cannibalized, interiorized, spiritualized, and this spirit that henceforth orders his singular destiny speaks not with the universal voice of law, but the singular voice of oracles. His mission will be decreed not by the law inscribed and monumentalized on the stone tables of a State, but by the listings of the spirit of the dead one inside him for which magic stones, fossils bearing the imprint of monsters from the primal oceans which have waited for him in the mountains raised by the cataclysmic upheavals which created Irian, serve as receptors. The cannibalism would then not be a eucharist which founds a legislated association, the pact of a brotherhood, would not be a participation in the mystical body of the idealized father which puts the legislator of the universal law in each one; it is a singularizing initiation by which one that has killed one of his own kind removes himself from the codes of association.[9] The word that now speaks in him is not the imperative of discourse which prohibits immediate gratification, addresses the libido to the other and regulates its articulation into multiple ways of symbolism; it is rather the breath and the power, the spirit, that issues the war-cry.

The war-cry is not a symbolism by which culture is constituted and a group communicates; it is provocation, insult, refusal of every response, verbal aggression against signs and against speech. It is the obsessively reiterated and exultant consecration of the decomposition of the species. It scans the disintegration of the code; it is, positively, the enhancing, emblazoning, magnifying of the singular one, it is the aural image of the solar being, the one that exists in radiant squandering of an incessantly produced redundance in the abysses of death.

The cannibalism then would not realize the internalization of authority, the subjection to the ideal ego, the castration of nature and the interminable symbolic articulation of desire; it would rather definitively singularize the killer, constitute the monster. Once thus initiated, he will live not to massacre humans for any economic, ethnic or imperial cause, but to hunt the jungle while the women garden and gather for food. For this hunt too is cannibalism; he hunts the birds and beasts of prey not to nourish the human family but to incorporate resplendent and ferocious spirits of the jungle. His worth is not formulated in the phallic economies of kinship, wealth, language. His war-cry is not a return of the repressed, summoning fraternal insurrection against the paternal interdiction that had silenced the original and absolute demand, the demand put on the other for total satisfaction. The headhunter runs in the equatorial disorder of the jungle, materialization of the floating minus-zero phallic signifier, eloquence of the absolute character of a demand put on himself, demand for singularity, for magnification, for splendor, integral monstrosity.

Notes

1. Claude Lévi-Strauss, "Introduction à l'oeuvre de Marcel Mauss," in Marcel Mauss, *Sociologie et anthropologie* (Paris: P.U.F., 1960), pp. xli-lii.

2. Sigmund Freud, *Beyond the Pleasure Principle,* The Standard Edition, Vol. XVIII (London: Hogarth, 1955), pp. 14-17.

3. Jacques Lacan, *Ecrits, A Selection*, trans. Alan Sheridan (New York: Norton, 1977), pp. 318-319.

4. Ibid., p. 311.

5. Ibid., pp. 2-4.

6. The cannibalistic lust of the infant seeking to devour the whole mother, and not only the breast, can only be a phantasm. It is not this cannibalism that is institutionalized.

7. Jacques Lacan (above, note 3), p. 820.

8. Pierre Klossowski, *Sade mon prochain, précédé de Le philosophe scélerat* (Paris: Seuil, 1967), pp. 31-37.

9. The "non-eucharistic" character of cannibalism in Irian makes it intelligible that it could be, as in the Dani Valley, abandoned even without the threats of Dutch guns or prisons.

Tantra

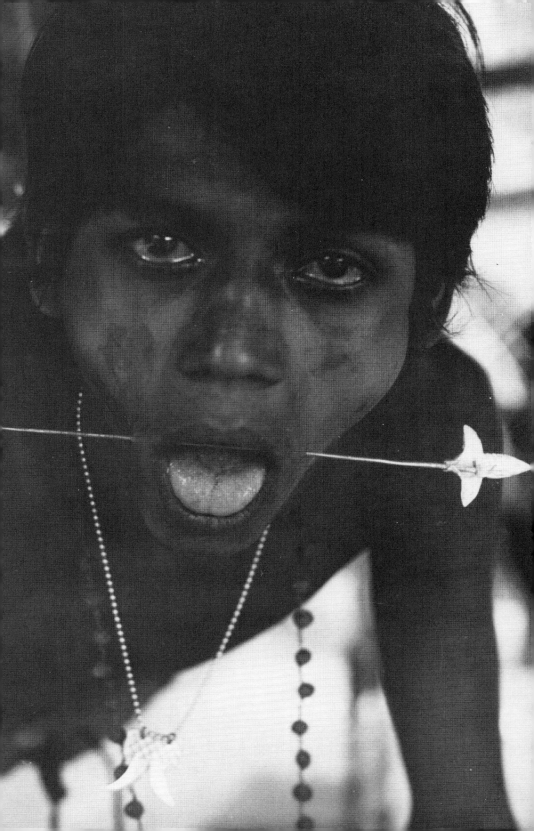

A MAN CAN BE A SIGN.

From measurable and from uncharted distances, another's alien existence can concern us, can contest us. What suffers in him can seem to us the cipher of an order that commands us. Yet one can use the other—the dreamer, those that live in the Easts, those without personality, suppliers of raw material for the West and raw material themselves—for entertainment, for instruction, for enrichment, for the exercise of one's sovereignty. Western sovereignty, sovereignty of reason.

For there is sovereignty in thought. Mortal sovereignty. Phallic sovereignty.

An imperative weighs on thought. The force of law, Kant wanted us to see, is a fact. It is the first fact: facts can be conceived as facts in the measure that they can be apprehended by a thought ordered by law. Thought is obedience. Concepts of what is always and everywhere found in things, propositions formulating what has to be understood as connected, are formed by a mind that is subject to law, and because it is.

One has no concept of the imperative force of law; it is not put forth by an initiative of the mind. Law is obeyed before it can be conceived, formulated, understood. It is because the mind's substance is receptive to the exigency for law that it can and does activate itself to think coherently and consistently. This receptivity, this passivity or this passion, this passive subjection which precedes and makes possible any consistent formulation of an act of thought, is an intellectual feeling, the feeling in which the intellect is born; Kant calls it the sentiment of respect. The mind thinks out of respect for law. Respect is, Kant says, something like fear, something like inclination. The law affects, pains our sensuous nature and our natural appetites. There is fear of the law in the mind.

Every animate being is activated by itself, that is, by its own representations. It has senses which form representations of what happens to affect them, represent external forms as containing pleasure or pain, which lure or repel the vital will. The mind obedient to law formulates universal and necessary representations, representations of principles, and sets them before the will, such that these representations function normatively, order the executive forces of life. The law is, in Kant's formulation, act in such a way that the maxim represented for your will is universal and necessary. The mind thinks on command, but it is commanded to be in command.

The will energized by sensuous representations is activated from without. The promise of pleasure that lures the will is represented as contained in the images of external objects. This will is energized by particulars. By the here and now, the contingently there. To such an externally excited, impermanent will, the sense of law opposes a will activated by principles its own representational faculty puts to it and a will activated by the universal and necessary, thus activated always and in all circumstances, always in act—ideal state of the will. This will is the Western will to be a person. A person is an ideal entity, that is, one that maintains itself in force. The will to be a person is produced by thought, by subjection to law.

Kant has explained how this will requires certain images. The imperative that commands the rational mind, that it command the will, demands that contingent external things no longer be taken as ends for the will. Nature is to be envisaged not as a domain of pleasures that captivate the sensuous will—ends—but as so much material to be ordered by the decrees of the rational will in us—means only. Our rational mind and will must no longer be taken as a means for the gratification of our own heteronomously regulated material nature. The thinking personality can be imagined only as an end in itself. And it has to be imagined as autonomous, like an independent political unit regulated only by the laws it has legislated for itself. These images give us a sense of the will to be a person as not only of value, but of absolute dignity, against which the worth of all things in nature is measured.

These images do not come out of insights we have into our own constitution; they are produced by an imagination commanded by thought. They are how we have to imagine our position in nature, and our internal constitution, so as to imagine ourselves able to be obedient to law alone. These images have not theoretical but practical value; we need them to guide us in forming practical judgments as to how to act in the world. The images have to be formed not by generalizing particular cases we can perceive, for in reality we have no perception of causality generally, and in particular, no perception of the causality that activates the will. We have neither perception nor understanding of the causality by which the will in turn could activate the nervous circuitry and musculature of our bodies. Hence we can never be sure that any given case of real behavior we can observe in the world, or any of our own actions we can perceive, is in fact activated exclusively by principle and not by external material forces or inner unconscious forces. The general images of our existence that give us a sense of our sovereign dignity we have to construct ourselves, by an imagination commanded by thought alone, which is obedient to the imperative of imagining ourselves capable of obeying law. Our person as an end in itself, and its operation as autonomously regulated—these are the obsessive images of sovereignty that we ourselves produce in order to depict our existence as one of unconditional bondage to law.

Thus it is not that we Westerners, perceiving the growing power over material nature which our rational science and technology are delivering over into our hands, have finally come to imagine ourselves to be absolute ends in ourselves, sovereigns recognizing no law of external nature or gods. It is the reverse: first Western man, who has isolated and made sovereign his rational faculty, finds himself unconditionally subject to law. And then he finds himself obligated to construct an image of himself that depicts him as executor of the law, not subject to the order materialized in the things of nature and in his own material nature. And an image that depicts him as operating autonomously, subject only to the laws formulated by his own mind. These images he produces of himself he carries with him in his enterprises of appropriation, exploitation and control; when he considers himself and his situation in view of action, he does not perceive his constitution but sees these imperative images. If he has finally made of his rational science and his technology the means for the reduction of the inhuman abundance of the planet and of the forces of the cosmic immensities beyond to the state of energy and material for his industries, that is the consequence of the supreme value the law of his thought has placed on his own person, self-legislating, self-maintaining.

I paid them to torture you, Prasadchandra.

Your black eyelids slide to open a little, light squandered by a star that burned out thirty million light years ago glows in the clove-brown jelly of your eye. You are five feet, six inches tall, weigh 112 pounds. Your face is angular, with high cheekbones; wiry black hair in sheaves covers your narrow skull. You are seventeen, still a boy, already a man, ready to die. Your skin is cinder black, blue-black in the hollows, moist under a thin mist of light. Your arms, chest and thighs are sleek, without body hair. Your abdomen is lean and bare, your navel set hard in a black rim on its surface. You are doubtless mostly of Sinhalese stock, but your broad flat nostrils suggest some Malay or perhaps even Veddah blood. Your fingers are long and thin, almost the same length, with long nails that flatten at the ends, save for the last finger on each hand where you have left the nail grow two inches, making your weakest fingers claws. Your teeth are hard and even. Your mouth is thin, but very soft, your red-ochre lips tremble like loosely attached petals. Your skull measures 42 cm round, mean for Sinhalese. There is thin stubble on your chin; the sun, a haze across your face, turns it into black holes or mica flashes.

You rise and walk out into the sky, white over the dunes. Your chest sprung broad, your arms set high and far over it, your narrow haunches and hard calves from a distance give a sense of great physical power; one is somewhat troubled then to see how slight you in fact are, and how soft and elastic your abdomen. When you pause your head drifts straight and far back above your shoulders, in the hieratic positions of Egyptian half-profiles. But when you walk your hard legs lift powerfully, and then your head rocks loose and diffidently to one side. Your arms tend to arch somewhat, as though ready to grasp or challenge, but your fingers hang loose on your hands, and seem to be continually feeling. Under your eyelids, half-closed, your eyes slide in gleaming brine, but not as though turned by a look tracking down something. Abruptly they close in over some drifting flake of light, like sea anemones attached to the alien body of the coral cliffs, contracting the mass of their tentacles upon a microorganism that is washed into them. Your lips are very mobile, the after-image of an inner smile often trembles them, but one has sometimes the sense of another expression behind, which even if it is not mocking the first is at a mocking distance from it.

Freedom, the causal force of the rationally legislated will, is not visible; it is known in pain, Kant said, pain of one's sensuous nature craving in vain the pleasure with which the forms of objects represented by the mind lure one. Freedom, or personal existence, is the negation of natural life, Hegel says, its mortification, the mortal sickness in the animal.

Cognition in us is from the first knowledge of death, knowledge of the power of death. Cognition begins in abstraction. It fixes this—this sensation—before oneself by isolating it from the rest, from the universe. To do so effectively would be in fact to put what is fixed to death, and thought has learned to abstract by learning to act, that is, to grasp, to dismember, to consume. The relationship of consciousness with nature is understood by Hegel to be one of opposition, negativity, mortal combat. To labor is not only to transform forms given in nature, but to consume the absolute being of nature, leaving it but a relative being. It is to transubstantiate nature into resources, means only, material for the rational ordinances of a will that recognizes no law but that formulated for it by its own thought. Spirit mortifies nature; freedom arises in opposition to the nature that is given in the here and the now and moves by evacuating it. It quickens the corpse with its own listing. Spirit is insubstantial and exists only in act—in lethal action; it lives extending its death into all nature.

Thought arises in the being that makes himself an abstraction. That sets out to exist for himself, on his own, having being as his own property. That extracts himself from the body of nature to stand over all that is given and to order it. To extract himself effectively would be to die, and the one that knows has learned knowledge from death.

What produces this abstraction in which one thinks and acts is the law. One does not know because one wants to; one is commanded. The law is recognizable as death sentence put on nature within. Knowledge knows first death within, and knows the exterior with the death within. The universality and necessity of the law that afflicts, that abstracts, the subject is that of death; the inner evidence for the causal efficacy of the rationally legislated will is the pain of nature agonizing within; the power of the spiritual personality is that of the invincible sovereignty of the death with which it forms all material substance.

This spirit of negativity, this negativity which is the spirit, no longer lives for material sustenance, earthly food and safety and comfort, does not seek pleasure, or happiness. It requires truth. It seeks visibility, declares itself, demands recognition.

You rise purified out of the sea as the last star parts into light, Prasadchandra, and the golden mantra AUM opens you to the roar of the tide. You look out over the fluttering dove-gray waters and the islands beyond and the mountains behind, the compass of the great mandala. You look through the dawn that blazes upon the tracks of the planets that have not wandered from their orbits, and beyond the fullness of the light always in excess of what eye can see you see the remote suns rage in the emptiness. You scale the outer ramparts of the cosmic mandala, passing through wall after wall, all the gravity of your substance seeking the core, all the elevation of your body seeking the central axis. At length Mount Meru, pivot of all the Himalayas, rises in your spine. Now the sea breath moves of itself into your lungs, your body has become a corpse. All human shape, the diagrams for human standing, human sitting, human walking, human grasping have left your substance. The worms have already reincarnated it, it clings to the earth with the spring of the locust, coils and rises with the cunning of the cobra, crouches in the ferocity of the leopard, rises and soars in the pride of birds of prey. Animal diagrams of power contracted not out of physical necessity but out of love attain equilibrium, mastery, freedom in your body. With the stand and the perspective and the mantra of powerful forms of life your body addresses the fields and the seas before you.

But not to act, to grasp or to probe. You hold still, in animal positions that are so many forms of exposure. You assemble about yourself the darknesses that press upon maggots, the great heats that burn the backs of lizards, the weight of years that lie on the bones of elephants, the storms that advance upon the circling eagles. Your tortoise, viper, stag, owl body in an insatiable thirst of suffering bears the terrible cosmic weight; you are a nameless fetus in the hemorrhages of the womb. *Mahakaruna*, the compassion.

A held tone takes possession of you, a chord composed of countless elements whose sustained power about the concentric walls of the great mandala pours into you. The circle of lucidity within you descends down the sushumna, the inner channel of your spine, to the muladhara chakra, located at the base of your pelvis, in the perineum just in front of the anus. There slumbers the serpent coiled about an inner lingam, covering its mouth with hers. What awakens her is the cosmic mandala you make pivot upon this chakra, wheel, of your body. A violent sensation burns in the circuitry of your genitals. The kundalini pierces the base of the sushumna. There is no ejaculation. The pounding in your penis builds and surges upward through the sponges, gorgonians, coral reefs, tide pools of your body. Your lower abdomen shudders, you feel the current turning in the second wheel.

With neither apprehension nor expectation you watch the on-coming of the new thrust, and you do not cling to it as it subsides. The inner conflagration leaps to the solar plexus, and flames in the spirals of the six petaled lotus. *Surya namaskar.* You adore the sun, adore its compulsion to lavish its energies in the dark voids from which no return is to be anticipated.

Under a blanket of grayness the sea shines like milk and mother-of-pearl. The waters breathe quietly, like a great sleeping animal. The muscles of your heart tighten and strain in the hold of the vulva of the female flesh that besets it. You are watching only the rise and descent of breath, the sun dawning to a splay of creeping and splintering things, the moon rising over ashes and fervor, you feel the light phosphoresce in things and die, and you crave *anicca*, the impermanence.

The kundalini fire sears up your throat and turns in the vissudha chakra. Vajrapani hurls its fires across the space of the howling passions about you. Your terrible stillness is that of the storm center of scorching typhoons.

Crisp and golden in the indigo sunlight forty feet below the surface a manta ray swims up through the warm sea with muscular undulations of the ribbed disc of its body, holding its venomed harpoon at a 20° angle. An eagle hangs on the surface above, a silver flake on the chalk burnish of the sky.

The kundalini plunges into the womb of your brain. Beneath the long dark lashes, the smooth limpid spheres of your eyes, Prasadchan-dra, are wiped clean and cooled. The black holes of the pupils widen and close in response as shape and shadow are reflected into them. Within the transparency of the iris is contained an intricate pattern, like feathers of glass, finely contrived, shining.

The sun stands still overhead. Your brain blackens. On Mount Meru, Shiva Nataraj dances breaking the circular course of the cosmic Ganges that its waters be squandered on this planet. *Anatta,* the no-self.

The person is a contingency, an entity struck with mortality, where a particular wills to be the locus of the universal and the necessary. The animal through which all animals die and in which all animality dies does not seek a term to this isolation and this death; he wills that they be universally affirmed. He seeks individuality, that is, in Hegelian terms, the synthesis of particularity and universality. He exists for his nature, particularized with the absolute singularity of death, to be recognized universally, for it to be reflected off the forms of all things and off the surfaces of all eyes. For all these reflections to reflect that which abides, the permanent.

The imperative, Kant said, is a command to command; one is commanded to command oneself, but also to command others and to be commanded by them. The very sense of the other, not only another shape of sensuous material, a physico-chemical apparatus, but a being one can interact with because he is an agent, is the sense of a will in him energized by representations of his own conception. The movements of an organism can also visibly be activated by stimuli affecting it from the outside, or by anonymous impulses arising within. The other exists on his own by activating himself with his own representations, representations not only presenting again or in advance external contingencies, but formulating the exigency for law within. To perceive the other is to sense the law that the other imposes on himself. To sense the other is to respect the other, to respect the law that rules in another, valid for oneself.

Thus for Kant to exist thoughtfully is to not take oneself as an exception. It is to not class oneself among deviants and aliens. It is to promulgate the law, for oneself and for everyone, whenever one acts. It is to make every move of one's life exemplary. It is to make one's moves such that they not only can be understood with the principles common to all reason, but set forth principles binding on all. Rational existence does not simply obey norms. It acts always to make itself the norm.

Spiritualized life is a force; it makes itself felt on the medium of spiritualized force; it forces the consciousness of another. In all the smiles of greeting, the words exchanged, the eloquence and the science and the wit among men, in all the libidinal and commercial relationships entered into, in collaboration, assault and subjugation what is being demanded of the other is recognition, acquiescence to the law one embodies. The recognition is forced. The free one forces his own command on someone that has the power to command himself, the power to put his own animal nature to death and to put to death that one that now issues the command. Freedom, Hegel explains, must demonstrate its existence to its carnal witness by putting the animal nature in which it arises to death, demanding to be identified by a deadly enemy as an absolute value. This demonstration, making visible, a spectacle, of freedom, is realized in the power the courage that the one that despises his life and has already consigned it to death has over the animal forces of the one before whom the demonstration is made. His respect is the fear of that courage. Respect is respect for the law of death, the death that commands.

You went, Prasadchandra, through midnight to the cremation grounds on the banks of the Ganga. You put your hand in the ashes of pyres and rubbed burnt sandlewood and burnt blood over your young skin. The Ganga below flows with ashes, liquified glaciers and stars. You have watched infants, the syphilitic, the murdered brought here. You have watched the fires climb out of the arms of the dead trees and turn leprous the stomachs and the faces of bankers, soldiers, and priests. You watched until you no longer could say whether the fire blazing in your eyes was watching the incineration of corpses, or whether it was out of your own eyes, in your ash-covered nakedness, that came the fires that feed on all that lives. The cold jaws of the crocodile clamp in the river below. A leopard drifts soundlessly through the mangrove swamps. In the pale moon a venomous spider drops a magnesium thread onto a child sleeping in a hammock beside a hut high in the hills. You laid out your limbs as a cremation pyre upon which all that lives in you is to be immolated. You went to death as Robinson went to inhabit the innermost cave of Speranza. One must not imagine, Tournier wrote, that the blind live in darkness; they live in a landscape of odors, tones and reliefs. Remaining long in the innermost night of Speranza, the moment came when Robinson ceased to see according to the cleavage between light and shadow. "The darkness suddenly changed its nature. The blackness in which he was enveloped turned to white. He was floating in white shadow, like a lump of cream in a bowl of milk."[1]

The guru Krishnananda comes to you. He is grave and hard with the years of what he has found in the experiments he has performed on himself. Why do these years bind you to him? What is this strange and frightful trust, in the circuitry of his body and the singular drives of his mind? Has he chosen you to castrate, so that he could be put to death by your hand? Two skydivers jump from a jet plane flying at 450 mph at 15,000 feet; the first, only space-clad, will free-fall for ten thousand feet accelerating at 32 f/sec^2; the second, freefalling more quickly, will be there to hand him his parachute to meet the earth rush of the last 5000 feet. A seventeen-year-old Gilbert Island boy named Hanuman leaps into the sea and dives down to the lair of the octopus. His eyes meet the great eyes of the octopus; then the black tentacle whips around his thighs. Sixty feet above in the sun, Ram is watching for the exact moment when the force of the octopus holding his friend will drain from its hold on the rock. The octopus fastens its beak on his chest, Hanuman hurls himself with a violent scissors kick, the octopus lets go of the rock to clamp the body of the boy. Ram dives and bites the octopus between the eyes, sinking his teeth into the octopus brain; it dies instantly.

Guru Krishnananda brings you the outcaste woman. She names herself with the name of power, Sakti. *That power who is defined as consciousness in all beings, reverence to her.* You have never before seen this hair glinting blue in the glow of the cremation ashes, these opulent legs that wander in the wastelands outside of all social and ethical geographies, this mouth that has tasted every forbidden food. *That power who is known as reason in all beings, who exists in all beings in the form of sleep, reverence to her.* Jasmine are her arched hands in the yonimudra, keora is her neck, champa and hina are her swollen breasts, sandalpaste and musk her thighs, knus her feet dancing on the ashes of the corpse that is you. *That power who exists in all beings as hunger, who exists in all beings as shadow, who exists in all beings as force, reverence to her.* The flower animals in your inner coral reefs grip their shivering tentacles about her, all the vegetation in you creeps about her, all the serpents in you twist about her, all the birds of prey in you fall upon her. *That power who exists in all beings in the form of thirst, as forgiveness, in the form of species, as bashfulness, reverence to her.* You release in her all the powers of your yoga. You lay your corpse among the cremation pyres. Your lingam stands in the midst of ashes. *That power who exists in all beings as peace, in the form of flesh, as loveliness, as fortune, as vocation, reverence to her.* She dances upon your corpse, she says her name is Kali, Kala—time, she mounts your erection, and your semen black as tar covers the night with dew. *That power who exists in all beings in the form of memory, as compassion, as fulfillment, as mother, in the form of illusion, reverence to her.* Each time the guru Krishnananda has brought you a different woman. Since you were seven years old. Since then you have known no other form of woman, known no other form of orgasm.

What is the genesis of the mortal imperative in a nature? By what abstraction, excision, does the will for natural pleasures give place to the ideal will to embody the law? Through what reversal, what violence, does our nature make the mortal nothingness it knows ahead of it the power with which it lives and commands?

The Western psychoanalysis says: the imperative is phallic. The polymorphously perverse infant, without speech, without logic or law, becomes respectful. Respect in the libido is something like fear, something like inclination. The fear is revealed by the psychoanalysis to be castration anxiety. Infant self-perception is an imago of anarchy, of dismemberment. Anarchic infant perception will be ordered in discourse, through the paternal, that is, imperative, force of language. The force of the law of the father is felt in the pain of sensuous cravings rendered inoperative. The pleasure object interdicted is that immediately on hand, one's own body, one's penis. penis is from the first a detachable organ. It will never lose this character, arising outside of the voluntary control that commands the rest, stiffening in erection while the postural organization of the rest collapses. It is articulated or abstracted in discourse, singled out as seriously dissectable by the word of the father. The paternal word is not indicative, but imperative, interdiction; the word of the father is a threat of castration. It will be, Freud says, taken seriously by the horror in which the infant will discover the castration of the mother. The paternal threat of dismemberment excises the infantile penis from the body-image as a pleasure-object. In the body image there is henceforth the untouchable shape of a phallus, the empty place of an absence. The phallus is that which is absent from the mother through mutilation and abstracted from his own body-image qua pleasure-object through interdiction.

Something like fear, something like inclination. For the infant perceives, at the same time as the menace that weighs on him, the chance he is. He perceives his mother desiring him as a mutilated body craves the part detached, castrated, from it. He comes to will to be the phallus the mother craves, to will to exist as that which orders all the desires of the other. Seeing the mutilation of the mother, recognizing the seriousness of the paternal threat, is recognizing the possibility of reformulating his own body-image, castrated, detached from his own pleasure, as imperative, as universal norm. The child sacrifices the desire to have the particular pleasure object of his own penis, but does so because this particular craving gives way before the demand for unconditional love his desire for phallic being formulates. A desire to be mortifies the infantile desire to have, the phallic will puts to death the infantile craving for an end to suffering, that is, for masturbation. The phallic will commands a will for castration—his own and that of the other.

The phallus, abstracted by the word of the father and addressed imperatively to the desire of the other, arises as a phantom of absence, a phantasmal image of the child reflected in the desire of the other. The craving to be a phallus realizes the abstraction that individualizes, synthesizes particularity with universality, makes one the singular will that commands every other, that is desired by every other. As a phallus, a man can be a sign. The imperious will to embody the vertical, the normative, statute, the abiding, the permanent, rises with the ascendancy of the phallic phantasm.

White flash fires are breaking out in sheets across the Indian Ocean. The wind advancing off the waves ripples the fields of sand of Sri, resplendent, Lanka. You, Prasadchandra, walking by the sea on a film of small white crabs. Plovers run about you, tacking against the advancing surf. Wine-colored medusas covered with pale amber spots gleam in the foam, pulsating their eyeless agony in the lethal light. The plovers do not pause before them, there are no flies collecting on them. The medusas, animals that cannot produce any action, have spent their lives filling themselves with venom. This poison is their consciousness. The ocean advances and recedes over the silver dunes of skeletons made by the flower animals and over the voiceless agony of the medusas. You walk in the film of water the receding tide leaves over them, glazing the rim of land with the clouds. You have walked all day on this film of sky, thick with white crabs.

Darkness is coming down like rain between the black pennants of the banana trees. You walk into the laughter at Hikkaduwa. Fires are burning here and there, and groups of long-legged Australians are lying across the vast horizontality, spreading their thighs for Dravidian women and electronic songs to massage. Some Norwegian nurses in rose skin flown in out of the big darkness north are forgetting the ones with pustulant tumors, the cantankerous terminally cancered, the snarlings of senility. Tropical forgetting. You walk among them, looking at the different colors of pubic hair, the great size of the white penises, the wide girth of pelvises shaking with the white laughter. You do not try to understand the language, hearing instead the sheen or color with which so many grammars of expression polish laughter.

You recognize a girl you spoke with yesterday, driven to Hikkaduwa by the four-month's dryness northeast, when all the land is dust and all the wells are empty. Her cool eyes pouring over white flesh, her liquid fingers tormenting it with infinite tenderness, her young lips kissing what had never been kissed. I spoke with him yesterday, he is a personnel manager here to recruit laborers at thirty-five U.S. dollars a month for the factory the parent firm in Frankfurt is opening in Colombo; he agreed to give her forty rupees—$3.60—for the night. He is feeling tender youth pour over the weariness of the years, the transfusion.

The beam of a motorcycle splits the night, on it a black Tamil boy with flashing eyes and diamond teeth, handsome as Vishnu riding the back of Garuda. Born in your village, Prasadchandra, he knows all the languages the Maharaja of Kandy knew, and German, French and English, and he plays the veena and has mastered the arts of the Kamasutra as well as those of Munich and San Francisco. Fifth son of his father, there had been no more paddy land to divide. An untouchable, he had been hired to clean the toilets of the Coral Gardens Hotel, at a salary of thirteen dollars a month, toilets adjoining the lusty white rooms.

Four rickshawallahs surround a laughing white man. They are making him the offering of a virgin. He is bargaining with his fingers. "*Zehn dollar nein! Fünf dollar!*" not because it really interests him to try to reduce the cost price in half, earning as he does in Munich what works out to $217 an eight-hour day, but bargaining to enter into the practices of the local culture, good-naturedly. The rickshawallah will transport him down the road for ten minutes, then stop before a taxi, and ask for ten rupees. The white man will grumble some, for the culture, good-naturedly, give him ten rupees and climb into the taxi. The driver will drive him for ten minutes, then stop in the darkness, and will ask for fifty rupees. The white man will shrug his shoulders, laugh good-naturedly, give him fifty rupees and sit in another ricksha and get pulled for ten minutes. They will stop before another ricksha with the curtain dropped down. The white man will climb into it, between two thin bodies. "Chose," they laugh. He will laugh and choose both. The rickshawallah will pull them for ten minutes, then stop before a house. The white man will give the ricksha man ten rupees, then thirty rupees to the man who will show him a cubicle, four rupees to the boy who will bring him a piece of soap, and three rupees to the girl who will bring him a pot of water. Then he will push his white penis through the thin wall of the hymen.

You turn into the trees, Prasadchandra, and move silently through the powdery moths. On Pidurutalagala an elephant lumbering through the night rears with its trunk around the kicking torso of his mahout and hurls him into the rock cliff. In Wilpattu four men are sawing off the horn of the white rhinoceros. You stop under a bodhi tree, and close the black leaves over the cinders of your eyes. Men in dirty lungis are lighting torches. In the midst of the night, another night falls upon you like rain. From within a terrible fear clamps you. You hold the fear like in the sea a medusa filled with brine.

In all the spheres of culture in which signs—women, wealth, messages—circulate, that which commands—the craving for upright thinking, for ordered sensibility and rectitude in judgment, for unequivocal identity, for consistency, for physical integrity and psychic normality—is phallic. In all the capitalisms in which currency—women, commodities, messages—circulate among consumers, that is, subjects of desire, castrated ones, that which commands is phallic. Women, wealth, messages first become currency, signs, when they cease to be objects of immediate gratification, that is, among civilized ones, castrated ones. They cease to be pleasure objects to become signs by which a phallic will exacts recognition.

The law does not command hypothetically; the wealth of civilization is not given in exchange for a renunciation of immediate gratification. The one that is no longer an infant, that speaks, does not turn to the world of civilized objects as to what can remunerate him for a libido that has interdicted but not put to death its infant cravings for voluptuous gratification. The phallic imperative, will to be what is from the first pure absence, is not the final phantasm of the one who, through the renunciation of infantilism and savagery, through instinctual renunciation, has acceded to the throne of global scientific and technological empire, and can now liberate from their Bastille all his polymorphously perverse aborigine desires. For it is law that orders the world, that objectifies objects, that makes nature into wealth, means only, into currency, into signs. The law that objectifies them does not deliver them over into our hands for immediate gratification, for masturbation; it articulates them as signs, signs exacting recognition of the other, signs made into signs by standing for the master-sign of the phallus. At the origin of civilization is the incest prohibition; it is not set forth as the price one must pay for the pleasures of civilized commerce with the materials of nature. It is set forth imperatively; one is not left free to renounce the benefits of the rational subjugation of men and the willful conversion of nature into currency.

The clamp holds fast within, outside the dark forest drifts like the sea. The guru Krishnananda touches you on the forehead with his fingers in the yonimudra. You, Prasadchandra, rise and walk to the center of the flames, the tablas are thundering like avalanches and men in lungis are chanting mantras. You clasp your fingers about the Shiva lingam hanging from your neck, and hold it to your lips and kiss. *Bombolay Shiva baba alaknirengin.* In the mountains above, a rock covered with vines shifts position, and the eagles awaken. In one continuous movement you lay your body on the mat on the ground. Men whose faces are marked with the red and white lines of Shiva the destroyer tie your legs at the ankles with a piece of cotton cloth, and then tie your thighs together with a second piece of cloth. The guru rises beside you, you look upon him with eyes of insatiable compassion. He opens a cardboard box and lays it on the mat beside you. He takes out the bundle of five-inch steel hooks, wrapped in twine, and unravels the twine. He takes one of the hooks, rubs your back with the diagram of a yantra, then with a strong thrust he drives the steel hook into your back. The pain cuts into you like the hooks of laughter. Not a muscle jumps, the black lids rest lightly over your eyes and do not tremble. The guru Krishnananda drives a second hook into your back, on the opposite side of the first one. There is a sizzling breath like serpents in the darkness, the pounding of the tablas thins out and hardens in the chanted invocations. The guru has forced in four hooks, he runs the twine through the eyes of the hooks and binds them together. The men take hold of your thin arms and your bound legs and lift you high over themselves. The fire burns on the surfaces of your eyes. The guru stands on a stump and twists the twine around the warm limb of the bodhi tree. When he comes down the men lower slowly below you. The flesh of your back curdles as your body mass descends, then the hooks hold. Your hands are hanging loose, there is a black star sapphire ring on one of your fingers. You open your mouth and extend your tongue. The guru Krishnananda takes one of the steel skewers with the metal pennant shaped like a flag from Anuradhapura, and he pushes it against your cheek, holding with his other hand the inner wall as he pushes the steel point through, then through your tongue, then through the wall of the other cheek. There is no blood. He takes the other steel rod, and pushes it through your protruded tongue, so that the metal pennant on the end is flat against your upper lip.

Not pain as a transmission of vital signals to the central system; this searing torpor in which you are steeped reveals nothing in the secrecy it has violated. Not pain as a recoil from the foreign body in the organism. As though the body is no longer on its own, no longer maintains a space of its own. You are backed up to yourself, afflicted with yourself, unable to flee and unable to retreat, mired in pain, mired in yourself. The caustic density of the pain routs the ego in its last retreat. Not a muscle stiffened, nothing was confronted, nothingness was not confronted. The strange spasm of courage, which takes over and interiorizes death to make it the force in all spiritual force, is not visible in your opaque unfocused eyes. The invading density of the pain is borne in passion, that activity which consists in bearing its own passivity, and in the complacency of compassion. A man blinded in the caverns of Speranza, you live in a world of odors, tones, reliefs, which you cease to feel according to the cleavage of action and suffering.

On your cold wet eyes the flames leap. The volume of the pain holds you in the opacity and gravity of your being. About this compression Mount Meru supports the striving and the suffering of all that is born.

You watch the fortuitous flickerings of the things washed as by the Ganges about the massive rock of this pain, and their impermanence refreshes you like the hand of the consoler, the guru. Each breath opens vast, far beyond what content could fill, as though immense space were given for thin flakes of the fiery night that torment you with strange pleasure and vanish. Had you not borne more than death? Is not death deliverance?

You. Prasadchandra. Who am I calling you? What inner clamp of autonomy, what agon of death with life, what figure of mastery beyond what eyes can see, what son of Shiva, son of Sakti, what strange boy in Hikkaduwa, what man already dead, what mankind now dead? Your eyes are blazing blankness, a terrifying insanity of searing yellow, raging and seething over an inner secret. *Mahakaruna, anicca, anatta.* The compassion. The impermanence. The no-self.

Notes

1. Michel Tournier, *Friday, or The Other Island*, trans. by Norman Denny (Harmondsworth: Penguin, 1974), p. 89.

Cargo Cult

WILL I SPEAK THE TRUTH TO YOU? TO YOU, DEVIKA?

Through speech one comes into the presence of the other, in his alterity. Perception, feeling, even sympathetic or empathetic feeling, and action, even collaboration, may remain on the phenomenal surfaces, where the other is but appearance and relative being. But genuine speech, which answers to a demand and answers a contestation, is responsibility before an appeal and initiative of justification, reveals the veritably other. This speech has to be itself veridical. Mendacious speech not only distorts the forms and effaces the significance of things, it obscures the visage of the other, even if it can be motivated only by the continual evidence of his presence. That is why, for Hegel, truth, and not only subjective certainty, is at stake when the other is encountered, and the struggle for recognition begins. It is not simply that truth would be defined, arbitrarily, as what exists actually for at least two and potentially for all. It is that the very perception of another is an acknowledgement made in speech and only in veridical speech.

That is also why, even though the other, to be veritably and irreducibly other, is outside all that is set forth and included in speech, still the very discovery and acknowledgement of this alterity requires that the world be set forth, and set forth in a true and total representation (true, that is, total, Hegel would say). For speech recognizes the other not by representing him to oneself, but by representing the world for him, by responding to his interrogation and putting before his judgment. The veritable approach to the other requires veridical speech, and ultimately requires the totally veridical, total speech. Crossing the whole world one comes into the proximity of the other. One advances, reducing distances, a quantitative problem, of miles, of years, of sex, of money. Not all of these movements into proximity are equally easy or difficult.

The power to lie, however, seems to be a faculty intrinsic to sovereignty, which is the power to conform oneself, and not the fatality of being conformed, to the course of the world. Mendacity does not preclude a veritable relationship with the veritable layout of the world, since it presupposes it and goes beyond it. But it does nullify the relationship with the other. One cannot retreat behind one's opaqueness and travesties, and still retain intact one's perception of the other. For the other, in his alterity, is not a datum of perception, but is present only as an appeal answered, a contestation recognized, in an *apologia pro vita sua*.

Naturally I did not say I wanted to get close to you, Devika. I said I was looking for the Amri Yahyah, the best, batik workshop. Words that say that I want to spend surplus money, and that I know how to get there by myself, knowing the name of the shop and being on the right street, and know also you will get a five-percent commission if you turn up at the door with me in hand. To say all that in one word, I could have said to you I was American. But, to be understood, I said I was Belgian, Latvian, Etruscan. You told me you were a. dancer in the *wayang wong*. Is that an occupation? And aren't you at least twenty-two years old? Is that sleek face and adolescent breast due to malnutrition? When you pointed to things and gestured as we talked, your fingers fluttered like a Balinese *legong*, sometimes moving only the first joints of the fingers, or bending them back into such an unlikely arc. The Swedish girl had not been able to do that after three years in Suryabrata's class. I said I was a journalist, so as to say I had time to just travel in Java without being rich. I did not say I was a professor, wanting to discover Yogyakarta by night as well as by day with you, not closing the possibility of love with you. Three days later when I suggested photographing you with my journalist's camera, you said the guru had gone to Solo and had locked up all the dance costumes. Did you believe me when I said I was paying 5,000 rupiahs a night at this boarding house—didn't you know, from the room-boy, that it cost 10,000, what university professors in the Gajah Mada earn a month? You told me what it was like in the monkey cages of Sumatra, where women political subversives are locked up with their children. Was it youthful grace, the artist soul of a pretechnological Eastern people, the political passions of oppressed Java, the Oriental wizard intelligence that was so skilled in alluring me, that I loved in you, Devika? Did I believe any of these things? Were you real to me only in the continually rearising suspicion that you are not a dancer at all, not sixteen years old, not a Hindu, not a revolutionary militant? Did I want an answer to any of these doubts, since I compulsively told you I was older or younger, poorer, less educated, less knowledgeable about your country, more, or less, religious, political, libertine than I wanted you to be? What would we have talked about over a meal like I eat when I am alone, costing what you have to live on maybe for a month?

In Books Theta and Iota of Aristotle's *Nichomachean Ethics* the criteria and principles regulating friendship are determined out of a general theory of the nature of social bonding.

Association is not produced by simple juxtaposition; it is actual in exchange. The three species of *philia* are characterized by the exchange of goods—association based on utility; the exchange of pleasures; and the exchange of virtue—the association of those who, having functional excellence in themselves, are good for one another, and do good to one another. The telos of the association is not the constantly augmenting production of goods; rather the circulation of goods, pleasures, and virtues is the means by which association actively maintains itself. In the economy of friendship there is no capitalizing of wealth, no usury or profiteering.

Duration—abiding presence, constancy—is the criterion for the evaluation of the kinds of association in this metaphysics of presence. An ephemeral friendship, however intense—what Nietzsche called star friendship, that of those whose orbits make contact, but whom the eternal necessity of each having his own orbit will take apart again—will for that reason be inferior. It is also why Aristotle can write that the friendship of witty people is superior to the relationship between lover and beloved. When the bloom of youth passes, the pleasure the sight of the beloved gave passes too; but two loquacious friends can exchange wit indefinitely.[1] Duration is also the argument for the superiority of friendship among the virtuous over that among adventurers or rascals. "Only the friendship of good men is proof against slander. For a man does not easily trust anyone's word about a person whom he has himself tried and tested over a long period of time... In other kinds of friendship, however, there is no safeguard against slander and lack of trust."[2]

An association endures through its inner activity, which is the circulation of goods, pleasures, or virtues. The circulation can continue inasmuch as each movement of goods, pleasures, or virtues is compensated for; whence the principle of equality. The exchange is rational, is reckoned. "Both partners receive and wish the same things from and for one another, or they exchange one thing for another, for instance, pleasure for material advantage."[3]

In association between unequals—youth and elder, husband and wife, ruler and subject—it is reckoning of proportion that permits maintaining the principle of equality. Money is the means for the equalization. "For a comunity is not formed by two physicians, but by a physician and a farmer, and, in general, by people who are different and unequal. But they must be equalized; and hence everything that enters into an exchange must somehow be comparable." "Now, in these cases money has been devised as a common measure, and, consequently, money is the standard to which everything is related and by which everything is measured."[4] But Aristotle also sees honor as a means of equalization. "The person who has profited in money or in excellence must give honor in return."[5] Honor can be regarded as a sort of wealth, a social currency. A man's word (of honor) is as good as gold. Affection, too, can be measured, and enter into the calculus of proportion. "In all friendships which involve the superiority of one of the partners, the affection, too, must be proportionate: the better and more useful partner should receive more affection than he gives... For when the affection is proportionate to the merit of each partner, there is in some sense equality between them."⁶ Aristotle reasons then that we do not in fact want for our friends the greatest of goods, namely, to be gods; between gods and men the disparity of goods is so great that proportion in exchange can no longer be maintained. Friendship is wishing goods for and also from one's friends. "Consequently, one will wish the greatest good for his friend as a human being. But perhaps not all the greatest goods, for each man wishes for his own good most of all."⁷

Aristotle locates three cases of inherent limit, where associations are so unequal that all the money, honor and affection one party has at his disposal cannot equalize it, such that he is condemned to be a debtor always. These are the relationship between a man and a god, the relationship between a son and his father ("nothing a son may have done to repay his father is a worthy return for everything his father has provided for him, and therefore he will always be in his debt"⁸), and the relationship of a student with his philosophy teacher.

Aristotle thus shows association to be intelligible as a closed system of exchanges, governed by the law of recompense. It is precisely as such that it can be seen to be natural. The social order, maintaining its identity through its intrinsic and essential *energeia*, is like an organism, like a cell. Such an association fits into nature. For the cosmos, viewed in its widest dimensions, is composed of such systems, and is itself such a system.

Friendship, being a member of such a social field, is the essential structure of happiness. The happy life is active in its own functional excellence, whose sovereign and self-maintaining *energeia* is not to be confused with the agitation of servile acquisitiveness, whose measure, poise or equilibrium, conforms it with nature. This happiness is an active, not static, harmony in exercise, in the circulation of goods, pleasures and powers, and not the quiescence of contentment.

Aristotle excludes the possibility of an ultimate conflict between the constitution of the individual and the constitution of society out of individuals in an extraordinary way. He speaks of a friendship with oneself. One is oneself then not a simple, but an association of agencies.[9] Aristotle does not see life as a bundle of wants and cravings in matter, but as agencies, which are themselves goods, pleasures and functional excellences. "To perceive that we are living is something pleasant in itself, for existence is by nature good, and to perceive that that good thing is inherent in us is pleasant."[10] There is exchange of goods, pleasures and virtues among the agencies associated within oneself. These agencies are not equal; consequently the exchanges have to be made according to proportion. There is a ruling element, an inner king, which has to be repaid with honor for the services he renders to the whole association. Then "all friendly feelings toward others are an extension of the friendly feelings a person has for himself."[11] Both the association we call an individual and that we call a friendship, *philia,* maintain their essence through an inner circulation of intrinsic wealth, rather than through pumping in their substance from without. When other agents bearing goods, pleasures and virtues are associated with this association of agencies the apparent individual is, any apparent altruism covers over a calculus of equality or proportion which in fact governs the association. "It is also true that many actions of a man of high moral standards are performed in the interest of his friends and of his country, and if there be need, he will give his life for them. He will freely give his money, honors, and, in short, all good things that men compete for, while he gains nobility for himself. He would rather choose to experience intense pleasure for a short time than mild pleasure for a long time; he would rather live nobly for one full year than lead an indifferent existence for many; and he would rather perform one great and noble act than many insignificant ones... A good man would freely give away his money if it means that his friends would get more, for in this way the friend's gain is wealth, while his own is nobility, so that he assigns the greater good to himself. He acts in the same way when it comes to honor and public office; he will give these freely to his friend, since that will bring him nobility and praise... It is even possible that he lets his friend perform actions which he intended to perform himself, and that he actually finds it nobler to be the cause of his friend's action than to act himself. So we see that in everything praiseworthy a man of high moral standards assigns himself the larger share of what is noble."[12]

How could I sleep in a bed in Calcutta?

It was dark, Arun, when I arrived at Dumdum airport, and raining. A white man invited me to share a cab into the city with him, a British bookie, last clerk of the Raj, capitalizing the surplus value produced each Saturday by the industrial transformation of the raw material of chance. He supplied the name of a hotel cheap and centrally located when I asked; a scorpion crawled out of the cot when I put my suitcase on it. Then I went out to get a look at Calcutta before it all shut up; the hotel proprietor told me that Chowringhee Circus, the central square of the imperial city, was but five minute's walk away. There were thin crowds in the drizzle; but after a few steps I realized that all along the walls there were squatting or sprawled out human beings, some under little shelters of cardboard or banana leaves. With a few more steps my white skin had attracted a circle of black marketeers offering to change money, skeletal women showing me their dried dugs at which bloated babies chewed, lepers poking scabby stumps at me with tin cans tied to them, pimps offering me English girls or Eurasians convent-educated, or young boys. I recognized the feeling in me was turning into fear—not of these wretches whining their hopeless prayers—but of something evil and immense in these dark streets, in this night. The pain. I used to think that there was a proportion, that the pain was human, that if there was pain there was also a capacity to the measure of the pain. Like Nietzsche, who said that man is the animal that suffers most, but because he is the bravest animal, even seeking out suffering to his own measure, out of strength. In a half hour I was back, trembling, in my room. How could one look at, how could one comprehend the pain of that dreadful night? It was beyond all proportion, an abyss; now, here, five thousand miles away, Arun, I find I cannot even imagine what I felt and saw that night; in fact a week after I left Calcutta I could no longer remember or imagine. It was beyond the capacity of the mind to apprehend or the memory to retain. You, Arun, I remember, you softly said in my ear, "I give you body massage," and I looked at you, and wondered what you were insinuating with your hushed voice and big eyes. I looked at you and found you unappealing, boney and dirty and vacant. Every night you were there when I passed. Three weeks later I was already getting the sickness that was to end in those hospitals in Madras, but I did not know it at the time; I supposed that it was just another bout of dysentery that made me so weak and nauseous. That evening when I passed you I thought you had or could get dope and I wanted dope to get through the night. We went through the arguing over the price, I was bored and irritable and was only going through the motions, arguing over a rupee, which in my country is seven cents, but one has to keep to discipline, make the effort to frame arguments to your understanding, a rhetoric of persuasion to bend your will. One has to discipline oneself to keep within discourse and in contractual bonds. And so we haggled, and I refused you the seven cents, and then went off to spend a buck for *Time* magazine and go to my hotel room where I got fucking sick smoking your dope and puked half the night. That is why when I saw you the next night you had gone up in my eyes, having outwitted me, and I lingered with you as you insinuated slyly other ways you could be of service to me, wondering if it was opium or virgin girls or yourself that might be my vice. I strung you on, so that I could find the natural moment to invite you to sit down to a meal on me, and that is when I learned you were from Lucknow, where my car had been demolished by a truck my second trip to India, and we remembered the dikes and the imambaras of Lucknow, and you showed me your cobra tattoos, and told me of the Naga shrine where your mother had put out milk for the cobras every morning since the day you were born. You astonished me by telling me you were twenty-two not fifteen, had a wife and two kids, sleeping in a doorway somewhere. I ordered the biggest meal they had to encourage you, but you only wanted some plain rice you said.

When, a month of sickness and two operations later, I got back to Calcutta, just for overnight, on the way out of India, how moved I was, you appearing there in the alley, greeting me with such a look of surprise and pleasure. You asked where I had been and what I had done, you wanted to know about the sickness, and said we could smoke a chilum, but I knew that your buddy slipped off to beg or borrow a crumb of dope, you didn't have any. And we sat there, against the wall in the alley, and you told me how, by night, to get into the Towers of Silence for the food which the Parsees leave with the corpses of their dead they put out for the vultures, how one rolls the tourists who are out for skin, where in the Maidan the addicts get their fix by having their forearms bitten by young cobras, there was not enough time in your breaths to cram in all the life you had to tell me. And I remembered, too, a time years back when, your age, I slept each night in a different flop-house on Chicago's skid row, the down-and-out-in-Paris-and-London trip, but, unlike you, me knowing there would be another trip after that one. And then you took me under the Howrah Bridge where the lepers were huddled to keep out of the rain, and you pulled out a blanket from the derelict boy you share your rice with when you have some, and you laid me on it and gave me the massage a thousand years of Lucknow caste skill can give, and sang me the song of the prayer of the blind man asking Lord Shiva to give him eyes so he can see that lord of destruction. And then my mind got all tangled up calculating how much I could pay you for this massage, what would be the strict professional price, which I could pass on to you without fucking up everything between us. I had lied to you which hotel I was really staying at, and you accompanied me back to the hovel I said instead, and after you left I went out again to the one I had really booked into. You left to sleep somewhere with your wife and babies in the street. I never saw you again, that night I slept in a bed, and the next night in New York.

Where I could not remember, and could not imagine the pain. I tried to talk about it sometimes. And sometimes they say to me, how could you stay there? They would usually put it that way, not saying, how could you sleep in a bed in Calcutta?

I did; and on the other side of the wall, in the street, you were lying on the ground. All I ever found to say, to those sitting in couches in living rooms, was that, once you have seen that, once I know you are there, Arun, is anything changed if I move to a bed a hundred miles, or five thousand miles, away?

One can vindicate Aristotle's concept of the structure of human association in three ways. Intrinsically, by taking all social structures to be semiotic systems—systems whose elements circulate because they are signs. Secondly, by exhibiting the philosophy of nature it involves. Thirdly, one could supply a transcendental foundation, where its rational order is commanded by imperative, rather than lured by a telos.

The possibility of treating kinship relations as a set of rules for the circulation of women, that is, as a sort of grammar for a communication system, a language, suggested to Lévi-Strauss the possibility of treating language itself as a system for the circulation not first of information, but of verbal material, possessing immediate value. For that one has to see words as poets still see them—not as bearers of an immaterial meaning, but, materially, as forces, as goods—as currency. "As in the case of women, the original impulse which compelled men to 'exchange' words must be sought for in that split representation that pertains to the symbolic function. When a sonorous object is simultaneously perceived as having a value both for the speaker and the listener, the only way to resolve this contradiction is in the exchange of complementary values, to which all social existence is reduced."[13] Thus the problem of the origin·of language may be resolved by seeing the exchange of words as an exchange of goods, of values—seeing it as a modality of the fundamental structure of social existence. But is not the possibility of taking any social structure as an economic system, a system for the circulation of a currency, itself based on the possibility of the sensible element being taken as a sign? For a sign is a substitute: it is what stands for something else. A system of signs is a system of regulated substitutions and equivalences. A general semiotics would then exhibit the universal laws regulating the circulation of goods, of pleasures, of virtues, of money, of honors and of affections—as well as of women and of words—in culture.

I am not going to try to propose that some or all of the elements in the spheres of culture could be brute facticity. Let, rather, the concept of a *trace* designate an element that is, to be sure, found only within the human economy, without being a sign.

A criminal, whose telos is the perfect crime, and not simply the release of unsocialized or barbaric force, acts to break an established order, and depart from the scene of the crime. But the disturbance itself remains, and can function as so many signs indicating a malefactor and expressing, to the detective, the identity of the act and of its agent. The criminal then acts to cover up his traces, so as to depart completely. But the deed passed into the real, and the precaution taken to wipe away the traces of the deed itself leaves traces. The traces a criminal leaves in covering up his traces are traces in the pure or purified sense we can now reserve for this term. They are neither signs not indices, and they are not inscribed by an intentionality; the criminal meant neither to express not to indicate anything by them. They are not made in order to be recognized and repaired. For him who comes upon them, they will mark the loci at which an order has been disturbed. They refer to a passing, that acted to pass completely from the present, to depart from the scene completely. The one who detects them recognizes something strange, not about to present and identify itself and not representable, but that concerns him by virtue of this disturbance and violation of the layout he inhabits.

Yet calm has returned to the scene; one can act as if everything is again in order. The traces of the transgression can be ignored among the debris of the world.

Of the affections, which Aristotle takes to be a currency, a social wealth, exchanged for goods, pleasures, functional excellences, money and honors, Nietzsche regards two of them—love and generosity—to be like crimes. "There are occurences of such a delicate nature that one does well to cover them up with some rudeness to conceal them; there are actions of love and extravagant generosity after which nothing is more advisable than to take a stick and give any eyewitness a sound thrashing: that would muddle his memory. Some know how to muddle and abuse their own memory in order to have their revenge at least against this only witness: shame is inventive."[14]

There would then be *traces*, in the social order, of movements that did not seek recompense, that only wanted to pass, completely, only wanted to discharge themselves, without return. Perhaps there are in nature, in which the social economy is painfully set, traces of inhuman, natural, compulsions that squander their forces, in the void.

In 1819, a British officer of the Madras regiment was tracking a panther in a stretch of uninhabited jungle in the Indhyadri Hills, in Hyderabad. About midday he came to the brink of a gorge, some thousand meters deep, cut by the circling arc of the Waghora river. One of the bearers caught sight of the panther on the face of the cliff, disappearing half-way down into the tangles of vegetation. The officer dismounted and began to descend the cliff wall on foot. He found the hole into which the panther had disappeared—but one side was rock cut vertical. He thus came upon the cave temples of Ajanta, a complex of thirty temples and monasteries carved out of solid rock on the cliff face of the Ajanta gorge, 500 meters above the river, by Buddhist monks 2,200 years ago; the falling mud and rocks and a dense tangle of vines and lianas had sealed the entrances for the last twelve hundred years. The excavators subsequently were to find frescos inside that rank with those of Fra Angelico and Masaccio in the spiritual treasury of humanity. There didn't seem to be any reason to suffer the rude four days' bus ride from Bombay; I took the plane to Aurangabad and a bus the 109 kilometers from there. It was the middle of the July monsoon, mud and water dripping over the cliff walls made the descent difficult, and down in the gorge no breeze stirred; by ten o'clock when the sun's rays descended into it, the heat made my head fevered and my heart pound. Then, across the river and on the far wall, I saw the path. A footpath climbing up to the rim of the gorge, where a small roofed shelter could be seen, no doubt for pilgrims to rest in the breezes of the surface. I at once decided to wait out the heat of the day up there, reading a book I had purchased on the history, architecture and iconography of the Ajanta cave temples and frescos. I crossed the river on a vine bridge and headed up the steep path; the climb took two hours. At the top the breezes greeted me, and there was the little pavilion, with wooden seats.

There you were also, Mohan. When I saw you you looked up and said your name was Mohan. Crouched on the ground, your head wrinkled, covered thinly with strands of yellow-white hair, your deformed legs lying in the dust, how long had you been there. I sat down on the far side from you. But after a moment using your stick you pulled yourself over before me, and with an obsequious murmur of "Sahib!" stretched out your hand in supplication.

The sun was now high in the sky; no one further would pass this path before late afternoon. I could not descend into the fetid gorge again; and all round there was only dense scrub buzzing with gnats and, no doubt, malarial mosquitos. The afternoon gaped open. I had my book and my task, to understand the cliff temples. You were also there, Mohan.

I could give you a coin at once. But, be it large or small, what else have you to do, the length of the afternoon neither you nor I could leave and no one else was to be hoped for, but ask piteously for another coin? Were I rich as Rockefeller, would a certain quantum of coins finally slake your want, stanch the waste of your substance? Would each coin, held back and finally dropped, buy me a quantum of time to read five or ten pages, before your supplication moaned again under me? Am I to become an obstinacy, working in resistance of that cloying entreaty—absurd and hateful contest?

I decide to give you an alms—when I leave. Not a quantity commensurate with your need or the degree of your misery, but only commensurate with what my state as a rich and physically sound sahib requires. I am not going to dribble it out, coin by coin, at ten minute intervals. That is all I am going to be able to do for you. Why should it not be compatible with what I can do for myself—recover my breath, rest in the shade, read this book to learn what drove Buddhists to carve out the sanctuaries below 2,200 years ago? I will impose my own assignment here, there will be no exchange between us until I depart.

This plan requires that I command silence from the start. I can only refuse to acknowledge your presence and your supplication. I open my book. You are now beneath me. It is going to require attention not to let my eyes meet yours. You begin your "Alms, Sahib!" out of your ravaged throat.

You are not going to stop or go away. I take my book and move to the far side of the pavilion. After five minutes you have dragged yourself once more under my feet.

The afternoon creeps viscuously along. Never has it been more laborious to pick off the message from the marks on the page for hour on end. In this tedium I feel hatred for you, Mohan, over the pointlessness of the imposition of your despoiled existence on me. A scab-covered dog lopes up out of the scrub, and cringes at the pavilion, panting from the heat. You stir, you slowly extract out of your rags a tin can, and out of it dump some crusts of dirty bread.

And then my eyes know without daring to look that you are breaking off some of your bread and stretching it out to the dog.

The reduction of all social existence to an exchange of complementary values does not split the social order from nature; it is a naturalization of the social order. According to Aristotle, society as a field of circulation of equivalents does not only fit harmoniously, microcosm into macrocosm, into nature as a whole; it is itself a nature. That is, an individual that maintains its identity through its self-regulated intrinsic *energeia*. We can see in human commerce the rational essence of nature, a system maintaining its identity through an internal economy of reckoned compensations.

Aristotle's poetics assigns a psychological-cathartic function to tragic theater, and his physics replaces a tragic concept of nature, that which sees the force of nature regulated according to a solar economy, an economy of expenditure without recompense, economy of horror, that of the sun, hub of nature, which produces a surplus energy which it squanders in the void, receiving no return from the minute quantity which, far from itself, engenders satellites, wandering planets, their Apollonian-Dionysian life, dreaming and dancing life—which is only burning itself out as fast as it can. This expenditure without recompense would be the very radiance, the glory of the sun. And its happiness—"a divine happiness," Nietzsche wrote, "which like the sun in the evening, continually gives of its inexhaustible riches and empties into the sea—and like the sun, too, feels itself richest when even the poorest fisherman rows with golden oars!"[15]

How is this ancient dispensation—how is the glory and the horror—resolved into a universal rational economy of nature? We can now formulate it as a taking of the *traces* to be *signs*. It is done by taking the sumptuous monuments and the cults, the frenzied waste and the wars, as expenditures compensated for in and required by imperial economies, taking the phantasms fixed plastically in visual arts, the intoxications of music and nonteleological movements, dance movements, not as expenditure without return, but as catharsis yielding equilibrium, taking the games involving gambling and squandering of status, fortune and even life, the vanity of jewelry, the voluptuousness of perverse sexual activity, detoured from genital and reproductive finality, as festive expenditures that yield a return in the economy of everyday life. Aristotle showed how to interpret honor and affections as a social currency with which goods and pleasures can be repaid. All social existence is reduced to the exchange of complementary values. One does not recognize traces that mark the passage of the irrecoverable, the uncompensatable, absolute past, the horror and the glory. This operation of recuperation is visible in the interpretations of the anthropologist, in the tourist returning with a revenue of artefacts, photographs, reports, experiences, capitalizing on uneconomic social systems. But their activities are epiphenomenal activities made possible first by a rationalization of the social field, of glorious and horrible savagery.

Irian—"New Guinea"—how long the way, through its venomous swamps and jungles, high into its mountain retreats, to the Stone Age, headhunters and cannibals. The Dutch touched the shore to claim the west side for the Dutch East Indies in 1828; in 1884 the English came to lay claim to the south side facing Australia, the same year the Germans claimed the north coast. There were three stages to their coming; the traders, the troops, and the missionaries. Traders came first, to make contact with the tribes, bringing a glut of beads and shells, but also bringing steel axes. The Stone Age was finally over. On their heels came the troops, imposing an end to the ceaseless tribal warfare, or, more exactly, in very many areas, headhunting between one compound and the next. A few lessons showing what firearms could do did the trick in most places, and the patrols could move on, the populations apparently only too happy that the millennia of fear were over, and the isolation so extreme that on this island, in a population of a million or so, over 700 mutually incomprehensible languages had congealed, fully one third of the tongues of humanity! Then came the missionaries, and the single, limpid, all-benevolent divinity, the Gospel of Salvation.

The steel axe cut down the trees for the gardens and the huts in about one fourth the time it takes with a stone axe. But that is the main work that had to be done; once the trees are cut the planting of the garden, in this luxuriating tropics, is nothing. In socioeconomic terms, step one produced an instant leisure population in the jungle. The pacification also freed an enormous quantity of energy; one can think not only of the quantity of energy spent in the actual battles and raids, but also of that expended on the manufacture of weapons, decorations, the joustings, boastings, on purification rituals, shamanist trance consultations, victory orgies and funerals and self-mutilations of defeat. Thirdly, the redemption brought by the missionaries wiped out at a single stroke a dense population of totemic, ancestral and cannibalized spirits, all the juju demonology. Suddenly each mind was liberated of the occupation of being on the lookout for portents and omens, learning the ways of dealing with an unendingly complicated and capricious underworld, each mind having to decide on its own what fragmentary information is to be trusted, which comes from the white shaman and which from the black, each night's shadows, owl cries, serpent movements, dreams, fevers, having to be deciphered— suddenly this vast and metriculous ingenuity is disconnected and vaporized before a high noon deity which, if invisible and unimaginable, is nonetheless known with the simple certainties of the logic of benevolence, and requires after all very little of your time or mental energies, it being enough to assemble weekly about his white priest mumbling the Dutch, English, German, or Latin.

The three steps, these three emissaries to savagery, are of course not civilization, but only the preparation for it. What did the white man have in mind to do with the Papuans once brought out of the Stone Age, pacified, and saved? The very swamps and jungle had now to be civilized. The white superiority that brought the steel axes, the peace, and the salvation rests on an economic base; the pacified and monotheized savages were set to work copra, rubber, cocoa, clove plantations. Recruiters were sent to the bush, to explain to the big men that it is labor white man's way that produced all the beads, steel axes, rifles, cargo birds, all the excitement; the usual contract under German rule was seven years at ninety cents a month, paid when the term was over; under Australian rule until 1951 it was three years for ten shillings a month, paid also when the term was up and the debts, damage caused to plantation property, and medications issued, deducted.

One should not conclude that somebody was getting rich out of that—the Germans who were just as happy to get out when the motherland went to war, the Dutch who were making their fortunes in Java, or the Australians who pushed and shoved their ward into independence with, in the end, unseemly haste. What wealth there was to circulate came from across the seas, in cargo ships, across the skies, in cargo planes. Everyone ran up against the irreducible indolence of the Papuan. Some theorized that they were in reality debilitated by the malaria, biharzia, scrub typhus from all time, and, now, from the gonorrhea and the syphilis, but the medical evidence was inconclusive and most spoke simply of some Stone Age absence of motivation. Certainly the Papuans are broad and robust physically, compared with the Javanese and Chinese coolies the Germans and Australians resorted to in the end.

Fevers and delirium circulated among the rubber and clove trees. It was not to the plantations but to the bird-of-paradise plume dealers that the cargo ships came. Today it is to the preachers of paradise that the cargo planes come, their bellies full of tinned food, frozen meats, whiskey, CB radios, guns, live cows and horses, jeeps, film projectors, altars.

How long it has been since I celebrated Christmas, Father Coenan! I did not dare tell you. How beautiful your Delft chinaware, how delicious your roast goose, how mellow your burgundy! Frankly, I did not expect, on the walls of a mission house in Moanemani, a signed Appel print, nor novels by Kawabata and Genet, theological writings by Hans Küng and some of the philosophical books of Foucault and Derrida. How gracious you were to me, how much information you gave me out of your twenty-six years in Irian Jaya! Finally I ventured to ask you about the Cargo cults so much talked about—whether here, in your parish too, there were Papuans who gather on top of some hill sacred to ancestors or totemic birds, clear the ground for the cargo plane, gather around an altar with the effigy not of Jesus on his cross but of the cargo plane, manufactured with flint blades out of coconut wood, jabber meaninglessly over the open pages of Dutch or English Bibles pilvered from the mission, and wait. You smiled. At my journalistic tastes. You turned to Obeth Badii. Seminarian, one of seven in Irian Jaya, home for the holidays from the Franciscan Studies House in Djayapura, one more year to go before ordination into the Roman Catholic priesthood.

The next day you took off your mission clothes, Obeth Badii, greased your body with pig fat, put the *kotecka* on your penis, and took me over the mountain wall. For a week we slept in your village;

I tried to make myself useful, chopping away at the brush with a stone adz for a new garden. You did not answer me, Obeth Badii, when on New Year's Day I finally asked you if I could see the shrine of the Cargo cult. When we parted your brother Adof presented me with a magnificent set of Kapauku bow and arrows. Some for the hunt, barbed in different ways for wild pigs, tree kangaroos, large birds. Some for war, smooth, not poisoned, but with coils of orchid fibers wound on the tips, which will come off when the arrow is pulled out of the wound, will stay in the wound, to infect. I understood, Obeth Badii. I understood this was not a gift; it was an exchange. I understood I am to return to you, with guns.

The phenomenology of the Cargo cult is an investigation of the way the rational economy of the white man is refracted on the dark soul of the Stone Age. Its obverse, less studied academically, is an inquiry into the ethical impact of the destitution of...millions... upon the soul of a lonely traveler.

For us Aristotelians, it is among men who recognize an agreement, men with a sense of the contract, endowed with the capacity to reckon the equivalent in an exchange, capable of committing themselves, that association can occur. It is this good faith that one recognizes when one recognizes one's fellows. To recognize another is to begin something with him—an exchange of words, goods, kinship. It is to see the other as a sign, to recognize his significance in an economy of products, powers, pleasures. In the measure that the distance of disproportion gapes open, that the goods, powers, pleasures the other has at his disposal are the most unequal to what one has oneself, in the measure that there could be extravagances without recompense, the circle circumscribing the human community closes in, to exclude him. To the very measure that it is human, association is association of prosperous, happy, sovereign ones, masters.

The happiness of the human order, its equilibrium and inner *energeia*, is, according to Aristotle, natural; it concords with and is supported by the format of nature which is composed of such systems maintaining their equilibrium through an inner circulation of forces and resources, and is itself such a system.

Kant takes this naturalness, this significant structure of the human economy and this complementary form of nature, to be not a fact, but an exigency of thought. This happiness is not the motor force of ethical history. For Kant mastery is imperative; the mastery of those who can reckon and can recognize is something commanded.

Sovereign ones are not motivated by wants, appetites or ambitions, but by their sovereignty, which is for them imperative. They associate out of sovereignty, not to make demands on another, nor to subject themselves to the demands of others, but to command one another. What is new in Kant is the demonstration that the reduction of social existence to the exchange of the equivalent is imperative. As well as the subjection of all nature to the laws of rational economy.

The imperative, Kant demonstrates, is within: the faculty that recognizes and that reckons, rational thought, finds it within itself. One can not think. But if one thinks, one subjects oneself to an imperative for the universal and the necessary. Concepts of what is always and everywhere found in things, propositions formulating principles, are formed by a mind that is subject to law, and because it is. And one must think. If one thinks, it is not out of inclination or because of a project, but out of obedience to the imperative for law.

The representations of principle that thought formulates command the executive forces of life always and in all circumstances. Life is thereby freed from the bonds to the particular and the contingent. Sensuous representations continue to be formed, and continue to bait the will by seeming to promise pleasure or announce pain, but they become impotent to produce their effect. The visible and tangible representation of wants that appeal, of needs that contest, of lacks that put demands on one, of fortuitous riches gratuitously given one, cease to trouble the will.

Sensuous representations command the will contingently and intermittently. Rational representations of what is universal and necessary are valid and in force always and in all circumstances. The will commanded by thought subject to the imperative for law constitutes an agency, then, that is always commanded, always in act. The law commands first an inner transformation of the dependent, fitful, servile human will, that wants and that responds to wants, into a self-sustaining, self-maintaining ideal will, that orders. The rationally activated will is a sovereignty, an ideality. As soon as an imperative is recognized, this sovereign and ideal existence becomes imperative.

Invested with a command to be master, one is commanded to command oneself, but also to command others and to be commanded by them. The very sense of the other, not only another shape of sensuous material, a physico-chemical apparatus, but a being one can interact with because he is an agent, is the sense of a will in him energized by representations of his own conception. The movements of an organism can also visibly be activated by stimuli affecting it from the outside, or by anonymous impulses arising within. The other exists on his own by activating himself with his own representations, representations not only presenting again or in advance external contingencies, but formulating the exigency for law within. To perceive the other is to sense the law that the other imposes on himself. To recognize the other is to respect the other. Respect for others is not respect for their innate composite human nature, but respect for the law that rules in them. Respect is distinguished by Kant from admiration, for the force or perfection of the tangible vital powers in another, which resembles the sentiment of the sublime in physical nature.[16] The sense of the other as a person is the perception of his action as instantiating a law which is valid for me also.

Thus the others concern me, for the principles that govern their actions obligate me too. And, on the other hand, it enters into the very meaning of my own sovereignty that the law that I propose as a maxim for my own practical moves in the phenomenal sphere is a law I legislate for everyone. Acting sovereignly, in obedience to the law whose force is not physical but moral, precisely consists in not taking oneself as an exception.[17] It is to not class oneself among deviants and monsters. It is to make one's moves such that they not only can be understood with the principles common to all reason, but set forth principles binding on all. It is to make every move of one's life exemplary. The existence the law commands is commanding; it consists in deciding the law with each of one's words, gestures, and deeds. Thoughtful existence does not simply obey norms; it acts always to make itself the norm. Each of one's actions becomes juridic; one acts so as to formulate the law for everyone. Sovereign existence is an existence not only without particular, private interests, but without privacy, an existence through and through promulgating.

Through secrecy and concealment one aims at a private life of one's own, which is the direct contrary of autonomous—sovereign, legislating—personality. The command put categorically on rational thought requires that one conceive of every maxim put to one's will as a public law; the test of evil maxims is that they have to be kept from public view. Truthfulness devolves not from the material value of truth for theoretical and then practical ends, but from the essentially public, exemplary, existence the rational imperative imposes.

It then belongs to the essence of a rational existence that it sovereignly enter into relationship with others. The kingdom—or republic—of beings who are each ends unto themselves is formed by internal bonds; it must not be conceived as a simple coexistence of free and equal members, the tangency of whose spheres of sovereignty being "due to the roundness of the earth"[18]—as though if the surface of the earth were an infinite plane men could be so dispersed that community would not be a necessary consequence of their existence on it.[19] Rational society forms a "nature" through the universal laws that necessitate the movements of each of its members, but the universal laws are decreed by the sovereignly autonomous individuals. Each rational agent is a legislating sovereign, whose word binds all the others. The kingdom of ends is an association whose inner *energeia* is not the circulation of messages, but the promulgation of decrees.

The rational association of men does not then arise out of considerations of mutual assistance, for the reasoned gratification of wants is no longer the motivation of the will among them. Their rationality itself is not constituted through mutual aid, as though the consciousness of each could only represent the particular and the contingent, and the representation of the universal and necessary truth could only be constructed by the assemblage of all these particularities and contingencies.

If words, messages, circulate, that is because every rational word binds the others, because every mind that represents the universal and the necessary requires that the other mind likewise promulgate the universal and the necessary. If all the resources of the association circulate, if goods, kin, powers, pleasures given to others make demands on others, that is because they are gestures and terms of a discourse, not only in that the significance of each term is determined by its reference to all the other terms, but in that with each word, each gesture, each move, each sovereign one obligates the others.

Hardwar, the Gate the Lord has visited, the oldest place there is. Named in the Vedas, it is today a collection of temples and ashrams built at the place where the Ganges comes out of the Himalayan wall upon the plains of northern India. One can walk the forty kilometers higher into the mountains to Rishikesh, the place of the seers, where the Vedic wisdom, and India, was born. The Ganges, pure and green, roars through a deep gorge, on its way to the ocean and the underworld, bearing the waters that can be seen falling on the blue-white Himalyas above from the Milky Way, its celestial course. At Lakshman Jhula there is a suspension bridge of vines that hangs over the gorge; on the far side there is a string of temples and the huts of hermits, with sacred ghats that descend into the water; it is a place where pilgrims come to make their ablutions in the cosmic river. Not knowing how old I was nor how young I was yet to be, I went there, to bathe in the holy Ganga the first time in this life.

But on the way to the Lakshman Jhula suspension bridge I came upon the lepers. They are deposited along the path, some hundred of them. What to do? I draw back and wait. I see Hindu pilgrims, covered with the dust and fatigue of many miles, moving down toward the bridge, on the way opening a bag of rice and silently leaving a few grains in the pot of each leper as they advance. I am a white man, not a pilgrim, carrying traveler's checks. Give them nothing? Give them a few rupee notes I have? How? At random, leaving the rest to claw and shout at me? Finally I go to a Tibetan, and I change four rupees. The rupee is divided into a hundred paisa. The Tibetan gives me ninety paisa to the rupee, in two and three paisa aluminum coins. I proceed down to the vine bridge, dropping a coin in the pot of each leper, who glares at me with avidity, ready to shriek if I miss him or her. Even in India there is nothing made or grown that can be purchased with a coin of two or three paisa, equivalent to two or three fifteenths of a cent. At the end of the day the Tibetan will pass along the path of the lepers, giving them one rupee note for one hundred ten paisa. The paisa coins have no doubt never left this circuit for years, gaining their patina of bacilli from so many fingerless hands.

Aristotle thinks of the individual as an association which, through the inner circulation of goods, pleasures, virtues, maintains its inner harmony and its concord with the other systems of nature about it, lured by its own telos, and confirmed by its happiness. In Kant the telos of being a nature, a system internally regulated by law, found wanting in man and perhaps in the sensuous chaos, is imposed by an imperative. The sensibility continues to present to the will representations of pleasure which lure it; this sensibility has to be continually frustrated, the subjection to law will always be sensuously experienced as suffering. There are then two natures in question within the individual: the rational nature, governed by universal and necessary laws, and a sensuous nature, which has to be repressed.

What is the nature of the sensuous nature to be thus mortified? Our sensuous nature is energized by pleasure—but is this pleasure content obtained and contentment? Would we find at the bottom of it that pleasure that Aristotle said consists in feeling that good thing, that *virtus*, which is living itself? Is Freud right to think that the fundamental laws of pleasure are libidinal, orgasmic, solar, pleasure in the discharge of an excess tension, a surplus force?

Kant conceives of a rationally commanded agent as a nature, but also as fitting into nature as a whole, in that in regulating itself with laws universal and necessary for it, it formulates the laws necessary for the universe. The rational mind would be the locus of a destiny which would consist in formulating all the laws of the universe, and the rationally motivated will a force whose destiny would consist in promulgating them in oneself and for all sovereign agents. Is not this rational nature also constituted over the repression of another nature, whose traces, in the Kantian philosophy, can be recognized only in the form of the chaos of sense data which the mind will take as the signs of an objective nature? Could it be that this sensuous chaos the rational mind overcomes is the trace of the tragic essence of nature, economy of glory and of horror, solar economy, that which was disallowed by the natural philosophy of Aristotle?

If this is so, then the sovereign agent knows a conflict not between rational law and sensuous anarchy, but between a rational economy governed by the principle of equality and proportion, and a solar economy governed by a law of expenditure without return. For Kant it is clear that if there is an imperative, then what is imposed is lawfulness, that is, discharges of force governed by a representation of the universal and the necessary. The nature that is thus constituted, governed by universal and necessary laws, is one whose inner shifts are governed by an economy of recompense. Kant must have thought that gratuity can never be imperative.

I came to the Ganges at Varanasi, like everyone else, to die. Not knowing how old I was nor how young I was yet to be. There I knew you, Gopal Hartilay. You came to me at sunset, frail boy out of so many thousands of Hindus, each silent and alone, descending into the holy river to consign to it the sweat and dirt and fatigue of the day, as, one day, to consign to it the sweat and dirt and fatigue of life. You took me by the hand to the Manikarnika ghat, where among the garlanded cows we watched the fires whisper over the bodies of the dead, and the kites and nightjars circling overhead. One day you will be burned there, and your ashes swept into the strong arms of the river. You took me by the hand to your boat, which you tie at the Dashashwamedha ghat in the unlikely hope of enticing a party of pilgrims to choose yours from among so many dozens of larger, sounder, safer boats. As we rocked on the waters of the river you explained to me in tangled complication the epic drama that was being ceremonially reenacted by priests with foreheads marked with the mark of Shiva the Destroyer on the far bank of the Ganga. How little I understood of it; it was enough for me to watch your black eyes catch the last rays of the sun. When it got completely dark they shone still as you rowed back to the city, where we went to eat a banana leaf of rice under an aswatha tree full of sleeping monkeys. The clanging of cymbals announced a bride heading for her bridegroom under the full moon in a procession of four elephants, a white horse, a strident band, fireworks, and half the gods of the Mahabharata in effigy being carried along, and we went too. But we stopped at the Durga temple, where you wanted me to contribute something for a blood sacrifice to Kali, who took your mother and father with cholera the year you were born, but who wants you here still. How did I come so far, through so many dense crowds, to find you? What law dictated that you chose to be my friend? You clanged the bells loudly to alert the attention of the goddess, but alerted also the monkeys who stole the sacrifice and hissed at you from the temple roofs. We walked back to the Dashashwamedha ghat where you will sleep, having no room in a house and having to guard your boat. There were still fires on the ghats, and, here and there, solitary pilgrims chanting mantras like the names of the stars. I desperately wanted to give you a gift, and the gift I had in mind I would make with my camera, because it would be just you—images of you, images that duplicate not the frail and wild bliss that plays in your heart, but only a momentary look of your eyes, a breath, a shudder. I wanted to manufacture these shadows of you, I would have liked an infinite number of them. Not for myself; to give to you, because I could not imagine ever coming upon anything outside of you that could embellish you, my friend whom I found on the banks of the Ganges among the funeral pyres and whom perhaps I shall not meet again on this bank of life. Then I awkwardly explained to you that I had only a two-week visa for Nepal, and had to leave tomorrow early morning and could not drive through the thick of the city if I were to make the frontier in time, and that was why I wanted you to come to me, tomorrow, to my hotel, four miles out of the city, to come at dawn, so I could photograph you before I left. The next morning I got up in the dark, dressed, packed, had breakfast, waited; the sun rose, and there was no sign of you. I waited an hour, then finally got into the car and drove into the city. Half-way I saw you, in the crowds, on a borrowed bicycle, on your way. We went to the river, we went to your boat, to the Manikarnika ghat, it seemed to me that each wave of the river and each shadow of the city in which you glanced harbored an image of you; it was past noon when I got into the car to leave, and you accompanied me on your bicycle to the bridge over the river where we said farewell. Two days later, in Kathmandu, I took the films to be developed, and there was nothing on them. All blank. I met some travelers who would later go to Varanasi, and I made them promise to go to the Dashashwamedha ghat and find you, and tell you about the dead films. After Nepal I went to Calcutta, and three months later was driving back across northern India on my way back to Europe, and once out of Calcutta I decided to take the long detour to go back to Varanasi, to you, in order to see you, in order to photograph you. I arrived late in the night, parked the car at the first lodging on the edge of the city, and the next morning took a ricksha to the river to find you. But at the Dashashwamedha ghat you were nowhere to be seen, nor your boat. I asked the priests, bystanders, I sent off boys to look for Gopal Hartilay, I climbed up the Manmandir observatory where I could see far down the river, and at length I saw a cloud of dust and someone running and I rushed down again, knowing it was you. We fell into one another's arms, and had nothing to say to one another; to break the spell I said I was hungry for rice and asked if we could go again where we had eaten under the tree of the sleeping monkeys. We climbed up the ghats and suddenly you stopped and told me to go on, and after a few moments you reappeared, and you put in my hand a tiny silver statue, very old, votive offering cast into the river by a pilgrim perhaps hundreds of years ago, which you told me you found one day in the river, and which I recognized at once, and verified later by a jeweler, to be of great value. You could eat rice for many months, perhaps years, with the value of this. I looked at you, dazed, you folded my fingers about it, and your hand about mine. My head was dizzy; if I gave you all the possessions I had it would not be the equivalent, since I have a job, and more salary comes in, automatically, each month, with pension till I die. And then you vanished again, and when you returned you put in my hand some old Tibetan coins, currency of a kingdom that no longer exists, which you also found in the river. I looked at you with wet eyes and realized that's all there was. Orphan boy you had given me everything you had. And then you told me that the small silver figure represented the reincarnation of Krishna named Gopal. Gopal. Gopal is you.

Notes

1. Aristotle, *Nichomachean Ethics*, trans. Martin Ostwald (Indianapolis: Bobbs-Merrill, 1962) 1157a 3-10.
2. Ibid., 1157a 23-25.
3. Ibid., 1158b 2-3.
4. Ibid., 1133a 16-19, 1164a 1-2.
5. Ibid., 1163b 14.
6. Ibid., 1158b 24-28.
7. Ibid., 1159a 11-13.
8. Ibid., 1163b 21-22.
9. The ordinary English sense of the word "agency" is better than "faculty" or "part" to translate *dunamis*.
10. Ibid., 1170b 1-2.
11. Ibid., 1168b 6.
12. Ibid., 1169a 18-35.
13. Claude Lévi-Strauss, *Structural Anthropology* (New York: Harper, 1963), p. 62.

14. Friedrich Nietzsche, *Beyond Good and Evil*, trans. Walter Kaufmann (New York: Vintage, 1966), §40.

15. Friedrich Nietzsche, *The Gay Science*, trans. Walter Kaufmann (New York: Vintage, 1974), §337.

16. Immanuel Kant, *Critique of Practical Reason*, trans. Lewis White Beck (Indianapolis: Bobbs-Merrill, 1956), p. 79.

17. Immanuel Kant, *Groundwork of the Metaphysic of Morals*, trans. H. J. Paton (New York: Harper, 1964), pp. 91-92.

18. Immanuel Kant, *Metaphysik der Sitten* (Berlin: G. Reimer, 1916), p. 457.

19. Ibid.

Index